The Story of Mexico

The Mexican War of Independence

The Story of Mexico

The Mexican War
of Independence

R. Conrad Stein

MORGAN
REYNOLDS

PUBLISHING

Greensboro, North Carolina

The Story of Mexico

Benito Juárez and the French Intervention

The Mexican Revolution

The Mexican War of Independence

Cortés and the Spanish Conquest

THE STORY OF MEXICO
THE MEXICAN WAR OF INDEPENDENCE
Copyright © 2008 by R. Conrad Stein

Library of Congress Cataloging-in-Publication Data

Stein, R. Conrad.
  The story of Mexico. The Mexican War of Independence / by R. Conrad
  Stein.
      p. cm.
  Includes bibliographical references and index.
  ISBN-13: 978-1-59935-054-7
  ISBN-10: 1-59935-054-8
  1. Mexico--History--Wars of Independence, 1810-1821. 2. Mexico--History-
  -1821-1861. I. Title. II. Title: Mexican War of Independence.
  F1232.S73 2007
  972'.03--dc22
                                    2007022137

Printed in the United States of America
First Edition

For my wife Deborah and daughter, Janna

Contents

Miguel Hidalgo
(Courtesy of Art Resource)

ONE

The Cry of Dolores

F ather Hidalgo of New Spain (now Mexico) was a complex man. Outwardly the Catholic priest was mild mannered and bookish. Yet all his life he had been a rule-breaker, one who questioned authority. He defied his own church by stating priests ought to be allowed to marry. Hidalgo taught his Indian parishioners to grow grapes and make wine to sell to other people, even though wine-making was a trade forbidden to Indians by the government.

In the early 1800s Hidalgo joined a group of freethinkers who met in Querétaro, a city in central Mexico. The group had the innocent-sounding name of the Literary Club of Querétaro and claimed to be a reading society whose only purpose was to discuss new books. Secretly, in their closed-door meetings, the club members uttered a forbidden word—independence. For three centuries Spain had ruled Mexico. Now the men and women of Hidalgo's association pondered the radical notion of breaking the Spanish hold on their land.

Thus they treaded over dangerous grounds. Merely talking about independence in New Spain was an act of treason, punishable by death.

At two o'clock in the morning of April 16, 1810, Hidalgo was awakened by an urgent pounding on his door. It was Ignacio Allende, a fellow member of the Querétaro club. Allende told the priest that the group's activities had been discovered by Spanish authorities and several members had already been arrested. Allende himself escaped only through the courage of a woman club member who spread the word of impending arrests to other independence-minded conspirators.

Hidalgo rushed to the main square of the tiny town of Dolores (today called Dolores Hidalgo) where he rang the bell of his church. It was a Sunday morning, and his parishioners believed the bell meant they were being called to Mass. They had no idea the destiny of Mexico would be declared this morning.

Hidalgo stood on the steps of his church to address his flock. His exact words are unknown, but they became the stuff of legends. Outside the church, before daylight, Hidalgo issued the now famous *Grito de Dolores* (Cry of Dolores). The cry was a spirited speech which filled the people with courage and sent them marching on the road to Mexican independence.

Events after the *Grito* unrolled too fast for Hidalgo and his fellow conspirators to control. Hidalgo had envisioned a political, not a military, move toward Mexican freedom. The priest abhorred violence. He hoped his country could achieve independence through peaceful means, but the *Grito* had the opposite effect. Hidalgo's impassioned speech charged the independence movement with fire and hatred for Spanish authority. *Viva Mexico, viva la independencia,* (Long live Mexico, long live independence) shouted the men and women of Dolores. Then they added, in grim tones, *Muerte a los Gachupines* (death to the *gachupines*, a derogatory term for "pure-blooded" Spaniards born in Spain.)

It was as if the Cry of Dolores ignited the fuse of a bomb. After hundreds of years of Spanish rule, impoverished Mexicans believed they were, in effect, slaves to Spanish masters. On September 16, 1810, Hidalgo freed the slaves, triggering the Mexican war of independence. It was a violent and a bloody conflict, fueled by generations of hatred. The immediate aftermath of the war proved to be unsatisfactory for the freedom fighters, but the independence movement begun in 1810 ultimately granted the people liberty from colonial rule. The struggle for independence is hailed today as a shining triumph in Mexico's past. The war, though it was terrible, gave Mexico its greatest patriots.

TWO
New Spain

In August 1521, a Spanish army completed the conquest of the Aztec empire. The Aztec capital city, which the Spanish commander Hernando Cortés called, "the most beautiful thing in the world," lay in ruins. For three months the capital (present-day Mexico City) was the site of a violent battle between Spanish and Aztec forces. At the close of the battle more than one-third of the city's residents lay dead, and its once imposing pyramids and towers were leveled. A soldier serving under Cortés said, "The city looked as if it had been ploughed up."

The Aztec empire once spread over central Mexico from the Atlantic to the Pacific shores and embraced some 12 million people. In battle after battle with neighbors the Aztec army won victories. Then, the Spanish *conquistadores* (conquerors) came. Aztec power crumbled before conquistador horses, steel swords, and military organization.

The Aztec empire crumbled when pitted against the might of Spanish conquistador armies.

The defeat was so complete that as years passed it paved the way for absolute Spanish domination over the Aztecs and other Indian peoples. One Spanish priest, Fray Bernardino de Sahagún (1499?-1590), who admired the Aztecs, said, "The Indians were so trampled and destroyed, they and all their things, that no sign remained of what they were before. And so they were considered barbarians and people of low degree . . . When truly . . . they [were] ahead of other nations that are arrogant about their degree of refinement."

Quickly the conquistadors carved out their own empire, calling their territory New Spain. With surprising energy the capital, Mexico City, was rebuilt. It was now a Spanish city with churches, plazas, and imposing public buildings. Often the houses and churches were constructed with the same bricks that once made up Aztec pyramids.

The Spaniards spread out and founded other towns—Acapulco on the Pacific coast, Puebla and Guadalajara in the central part of the country, and Monterrey in the north. Spanish explorers and priests probed unknown lands in every direction from the capital, expanding the boundaries of New Spain north as far as the present-day American state of Colorado and south almost to Panama.

Other Spaniards undertook missions of conquest on the American continent. Soon the Spanish flag flew over most of South America with the exception of Brazil, which was claimed by Portugal. The Spanish empire in the Americas was one of the largest foreign domains ever seen in history.

Indian people in the far-flung regions of New Spain never fell completely into Spanish rule. In the north of Mexico the nomadic tribes resisted all efforts to bring them under the

European diseases such as smallpox decimated the native population of New Spain.

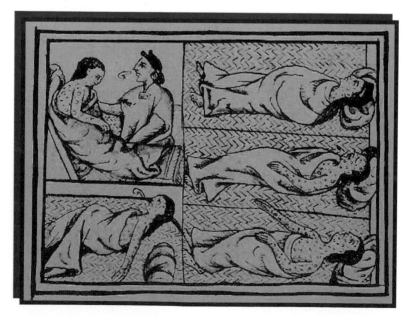

authority of New Spain. The Maya in the south acted as an independent body and paid little heed to government orders issued from Mexico City. Nevertheless the map of New Spain was imposing. In the years to come the colony became the largest and richest of all of Spain's foreign holdings.

The Spaniards unknowingly carried European diseases to the Americas. Illnesses such as smallpox, diphtheria, and measles had been in Europe for generations. Europeans had acquired immunities to the point where the maladies sickened them but were rarely fatal. The native people of Mexico had no such immunities, and the imported diseases killed them in staggering numbers. "They died in heaps like bedbugs," wrote one Spaniard. "And many starved to death because everybody was struck down at the same time and there was no one to care for the sick or prepare their food."

Depopulation

Before the Spaniards arrived in the 1520s the territory that became New Spain held about 12 million people. Then European diseases ravaged the Indian people. By the 1570s New Spain's population had dwindled to 6 million, and by the early 1600s it was just over 1 million. It was not until the twentieth century that Mexico regained its preconquest population.

The Spaniards also brought their language to New Spain. Before the Conquest some three-hundred different languages were spoken in Mexico and Central America. Spanish became the common language in Mexico, though many Indian groups held onto their native language and cultures in the face of the Spanish empire.

The people of Mexico once worshipped many gods. One estimate said the Aztecs alone had 2,000 deities in their pantheon. After the Spaniards arrived, Catholic priests lived with the Indians preaching Christianity and faith in one God. Priests also destroyed ancient religious shrines and statues because they considered them to be symbols of the devil. One priest wrote in 1529, "We are very busy with our continuous and great work in the conversion of infidels of whom . . . over a million people have been baptized, five hundred temples of idols have been razed to the ground and over twenty thousand images of devils that they adored have been broken in pieces and burned."

Priests were astonished at how easily the Indians converted to the new religion and agreed to be baptized. Many historians conclude the Indians readily converted because of the Catholic practice of praying to saints, which was similar to the Indian ways of paying homage to a host of different gods and goddesses. Also, many Indians secretly continued to worship their ancient deities. If they were discovered engaged in idol worship they could be tortured or even executed at the hands of the priests. Still, religious ceremonies took place in secluded spots outside of villages where buried statues of the gods were unearthed and worshiped observing the ancient rites.

The greatest boost to Indian acceptance of Christianity came when what was hailed as a miracle took place near Mexico City. The story of this miracle figured prominently in the independence movement and provided the Mexican people with their own saint whom they revere to this day.

In December 1531, an Aztec man who had recently converted to Christianity and had taken the name Juan Diego walked on a hill outside the village of Guadalupe, near Mexico City. Suddenly he saw a beautiful woman standing at the top of the hill. Rays of pure white light seemed to flow from her, arching into the heavens. Juan Diego approached the woman. Gently she spoke, in his native tongue, telling him she was the mother of all those who live on this land, and she

The Virgin of Guadalupe

wished that a church be built on that spot where she now stood.

Juan Diego hurried to Mexico City to tell the bishop there of his vision. Two things raced through his mind: First, the beautiful woman had brown skin like his own; second, the hill where she stood was once the sanctuary of an Aztec goddess. Juan Diego told the Spanish Bishop Zumárraga what he saw on the hill. At the time Spanish fortune seekers were running roughshod over Mexico—raping women, enslaving men, and stealing goods. Only the Catholic priests were in a position to curb Spanish lust and protect the Indians.

Bishop Zumárraga

Zumárraga wanted to believe Juan Diego's story because a miraculous visit by a saint would prove to fellow Spaniards that God regards the Indians as equals. But the bishop needed proof. He asked Juan Diego to bring back some token that he indeed had seen this saintly woman.

Once more Juan Diego returned to the hill at Guadalupe and again the beautiful woman appeared to him. She told him to climb the hill and pick the roses on the top. To his surprise Juan Diego found a delightful garden of roses at the peak. Flowers had never before grown on this dry and dusty

The Virgin of Guadalupe

Today the once tiny village of Guadalupe is a neighborhood of sprawling Mexico City. Highlight of the neighborhood is a revered church which holds the straw cloak bearing the famous painting. Thousands come to this church, some on their knees, to pray. The Virgin of Guadalupe is Mexico's patron saint, a special mother to the land. Practically all households have an image of her. A poor family will have a figure made of straw, a rich family a statue of gold. The significance of the Virgin of Guadalupe was reaffirmed in 2002 when Pope John Paul II canonized Juan Diego.

hill. He picked several roses and put them in his straw cloak (a tilma), and rushed back to Mexico City.

Bishop Zumárraga was disappointed because a few flowers were no proof of a genuine miracle. Then Juan Diego opened his tilma to show the bishop how lovely the flowers were. The roses fell to the floor and Zumárraga stood, stunned. There, painted on the inside of the straw cloak, was a marvelous portrait of a brown-skinned woman. No artist in New Spain at the time had the talent to render such a beautiful painting. No one—not Juan Diego, nor Bishop Zumárraga could explain how the portrait was put on the cloak.

Word of the miracle of the tilma spread throughout New Spain. Indian men and women freely joined the church after hearing the story. Spaniards began treating the Indians with more respect because the miracle proved that they too were children of God.

Catholic priests told Indians that Christianity was a gentle religion, especially compared with Aztec beliefs that

This image depicts the painting of the Virgin of Guadalupe that miraculously appeared on the cloak of Juan Diego.

demanded bloody rites of human sacrifice. Yet, in the 1500s, the church brought the Inquisition to New Spain. The Inquisition, which had swept through most of Europe, occurred during a time of religious fanaticism when powerful priests saw the work of devils everywhere. Men and women accused of consorting with devils or witches were tried, tortured, and often sentenced to death by being burned alive at the stake.

Immigrants from Spain claimed large tracts of land and became gentlemen farmers. Laws set in motion by the conquistadors gave white-skinned people easy access to land ownership. The Indians, robbed of land that had been theirs for generations, had little choice but to work for the newcomers. Spaniards introduced horses, cows, sheep, and pigs as well as new crops such as wheat, sugarcane, and citrus fruits. In turn, the Indians showed the Spaniards how to cultivate sweet potatoes, corn, and cocoa beans.

Silver was discovered in the central part of the colony in the 1540s. Soon New Spain led the world in silver production. Thousands of Spaniards arrived and many prospered by operating large farms and silver mines. Following Spanish custom, the rich families built soaring churches and funded universities, enhancing the grandeur of New Spain.

In the 1540s, the Spanish government passed laws forbidding the outright enslavement of Indian peoples. Still many Indians labored for whites, living as slaves in every manner except by name. To provide additional workers the government imported African slaves. By the end of the 1500s more than 60,000 blacks were brought to New Spain. A new race—the *mestizo*—born out of inter marriage between whites and Indians, appeared.

The mingling of whites, blacks, Indians, and mestizos created a host of people which the government called *castas* (breeds or casts). New Spain officials, who painstakingly put

The Races of Mexico

Mexico is a multiracial society, and the issue of race is also complex. The vast majority of people in Mexico are *mestizos*, meaning mixed race. But the country is also home to *indios*, (Indians, the indigenous people of Mexico), *negros*, (blacks, tens of thousands of whom were brought by the Spanish as slaves), and whites. White is generally used to describe Spaniards, and any non-Spanish whites are generally labeled by nationality rather than race: American, German, British, etc.

This eighteenth-century painting charts the variety of racial classifications in New Spain at the time. *(Courtesy of Schalkwijk/Art Resource)*

all people in racial categories, created more than twenty recognized casts or breeds. A person with a European father and a black mother (the reverse was unthinkable to the Spanish) was called a mulatto. Someone with a black father and a mulatto mother was a zambo.

Fear of racial mixing also led to two separate categories of "white" or Spaniard. Pure-blooded Spaniards who had been born in Spain (and therefore there was no risk of "tainted" blood) were known as *gachupines* (or *peninsula-res*). Pure-blooded Spaniards born in the Americas (therefore there was a slight risk of "tainted" blood) were known as *criollos*. The *gachupines* were the original target of the *Grito de Dolores.*

A complex tangle of laws regulated the life of the mixed-blood people and insured that whites reigned supreme. Only whites could hold high government offices. Indians and to a lesser extent mestizos were allowed to become parish priests, but customs prohibited nonwhites from becoming leaders or high priests within the church. Laws dictated the tiniest details of everyday living for the nonwhites. For example, mestizos were allowed to become mule drivers, but blacks were forbidden this occupation. Laws said that black women could not wear jewelry in public.

Castas were treated as outsiders and even as criminals by

African Slaves in Mexico

Slavery in Mexico was not necessarily permanent. Many blacks who were either brought from Africa as slaves or who were born into slavery could win or buy their freedom. This complicated the hierarchy of *castas* even more as "free blacks" were considered a different social category than "slaves."

New Spain's society. The *castas* were shunned by whites who thought they were untrustworthy and rejected by Indians who regarded them as foreigners. Many drifted into Mexico City where they were forced to live as beggars and petty thieves. One white immigrant in Mexico City wrote the Spanish

This painting depicts an interracial couple and their child.

king, "We are surrounded by enemies who outnumber us; Negroes, mulattos, mestizos are present in much greater numbers than we."

With few opportunities available to them, the children of *castas* often turned to crime. Cities became lairs for gangs of young *casta* thieves and murderers.

Despite discriminatory laws, one group—the mestizo— was destined to rise and dominate Mexico in the future. Mestizos were the whitest of the nonwhites and there- fore the slight favorite in the eyes of the establishment. Mestizos had more freedom to hold a variety of jobs. Many became successful in running small businesses such as grocery markets. Also the mestizos inherited some of the whites' immunities to European diseases, allowing them to become the fastest-growing ethnic group in New Spain. The mestizo population also grew dramatically because few Spanish women migrated to the Americas in the early years of settlement, forcing Spanish men to seek wives and companions from amongst the population of indigenous population. As early as 1650 mestizos made up 20 percent of New Spain's total population. By 1810, when the Mexican War of Independence began, mestizos were the majority people in the country.

Racial Statistics Today

In the 1920s the Mexican government quit the practice of placing people in categories based on their race. Modern census figures give no idea as to the ethnic identity of the population. Some estimates say nine out of ten modern Mexicans are mestizos. There are still many whites and a few blacks (again the precise numbers are not known) living in Mexico, but the mestizo is clearly the majority.

The 1600s is known as the "forgotten century" in many Mexican history books. It was a time when few products other than silver came out of New Spain. But this image of the "forgotten century" discredits the fact that New Spain achieved great strides in literature, art, and architecture.

Mexico City and other large cities enjoyed a lively theater scene in the 1600s. New plays coming from Europe were eagerly awaited events. Poetry reading groups were active even in small towns. Mexico's renowned historian Justo Sierra (1848-1912) said of New Spain in the seventeenth century, "It rained poets; literary fiestas were commonplace events

Inés de la Juana

in colleges and churches, and in them the audience was lavishly treated to poems in Latin, in Spanish, in Nahuatl (the Aztec language)."

Literary societies of New Spain were made up largely of white males. Mestizos, Indians, castas, and lower-class whites were denied school and did not learn to read. Schools were run almost entirely by the church, and church leaders were mostly interested in training future priests. Catholic laws forbade women from becoming priests, and even women from wealthy white families rarely enjoyed the blessings of an education. Still, Mexico's greatest poet, Juana Inés de la Cruz, emerged in New Spain during the 1600s.

Juana Inés de la Cruz

Juana Inés de la Cruz was a white (*criolla*) woman born near Mexico City in 1651. A brilliant child, she learned reading on her own at the age of three. As a teenager she entered a religious school and became a nun (*sor*). Her religious studies allowed her to pursue her interests in science and literature. Her passion was poetry, and her works became popular in New Spain as well as in Spain. Though she was a nun, she harbored a secret lover who had little interest in her. Unrequited love was the theme of one of her most passionate poems:

> Listen to me with your eyes
> Since your ears are so distant,
> Listen to my pen as it moans without anger:
> And since my harsh voice cannot reach you,
> Listen to me though you are deaf, since my
> laments are mute.

In 1695 a plague, possibly of cholera, swept Mexico City. Juana's church evacuated all its nuns out of the city to escape the danger, but she insisted on staying behind to treat the sick. She caught the disease and died at age forty-three.

Architecture was New Spain's greatest gift to modern Mexico. Towns and villages built by Spanish immigrants were laid out with streets circulating outward from a central plaza. Houses and churches were created with a blending of European and native styles. Justo Sierra called New Spain's culture an "intellect formed by the conjoining of two dissimilar souls." Spanish colonial architecture is prized today in cities such as Guanajuato, Taxco, and San Miguel de

Allende where laws protect the old buildings and forbid any new construction in the city center. Through its art, literature, and architecture New Spain developed a unique identity—a graceful mix of European and Indian creative spirit.

Leaders in Spain jealously clung to their colony. New Spain was ruled by a viceroy appointed by the Spanish king. Laws were issued by the viceroy and lawbreakers were punished severely. The Catholic Church sided with the monarchy on most matters. Catholicism was the only religion allowed in New Spain, and even the study of another faith was forbidden. However the laws did not isolate the people of New Spain, as Spanish authorities hoped they would. In the 1700s the world at large was aflame with new and exciting ideas. These ideas would eventually creep into New Spain and launch a drive toward freedom that changed history.

THREE

The Enlightenment

I n the late 1600s, the Englishman John Locke wrote philosophical works such as *Two Treatises on Government* and *An Essay Concerning Human Understanding.* Locke argued that human beings had certain basic rights that no government should ever take from them: the pursuit of happiness was one of those rights. According to Locke the primary duty of government was to protect human rights, thereby allowing citizens to seek happiness as was true to their nature. Decades later the American Thomas Jefferson read Locke. The Englishman's philosophy influenced Jefferson when he wrote the Declaration of Independence in 1776 and proclaimed all people have the right to, "Life, Liberty, and the pursuit of Happiness."

Throughout history philosophy has influenced political action. What begins as an idea in a book, translates into a movement, and spreads as a revolution. The 1700s saw a fountain of philosophical concepts spring forth, exciting men and

Thomas Jefferson
(Library of Congress)

John Locke

women and eventually altering the world. The era was called
The Enlightenment or *The Age of Reason.* Its philosophical
leaders included John Locke of England and the Frenchmen
Jean Jacques Rousseau and Voltaire.

The notion of reason was key to the Enlightenment.
Philosophers of the time believed men and women lived on
a vastly higher plain than animals because they were capa-
ble of being guided by intellect and reason. Animals, on the
other hand, were moved by fear and passion. During the
Enlightenment the question "Is it reasonable?" was applied
to all new ideas. Science as well as government came under
the scrutiny of reason.

The age-old relationship between kings and their subjects
was challenged during the Enlightenment. In the past it was

generally believed kings and queens ruled by divine right, meaning God gave royal families the right to have power over others. But was this a reasonable concept? Was a member of a royal family a more profound leader simply because of his or her royal bloodlines? Enlightenment philosophers concluded that monarchs had no special leadership talents born within them, and therefore the divine right of kings was not a reasonable concept.

Jean Jacques Rousseau

The political arm of the enlightenment was called *liberalism*. Political parties of various names were established, and those who acted on enlightenment principals referred to themselves as liberals. Forces of liberalism moved to dismantle the old forms of government. No longer would men and women accept the tyranny of a king, nor would they mindlessly obey the commands issued by a priest. Under the influence of liberalism, people rose up to demand rights and dignity. As liberalism spread, the kingdoms of Europe were shaken to the core.

In the 1770s liberal ideas entered the English colonies in America. Spurred by liberalism, English colonists ousted the government of the mother country and established an independent country—the United States of America. Liberalism stormed into France in the late 1700s and saw the people beheading their king and launching a bloody revolution.

At first New Spain seemed to be unaffected by the ideas of the Enlightenment and the power of liberalism. New Spain was a far distant part of the world. Even in the best of weather it took a ship at least four weeks to cross the Atlantic and arrive at a port in colonial Mexico. New immigrants traveling from Europe to New Spain had to have the approval of the Spanish government. Also, the government and the Catholic Church banned enlightenment books and discouraged the discussion of liberal concepts. In the late 1700s New Spain authorities put written proclamations on the walls of buildings warning citizens to stay clear of liberal thinking which was shaking the order in many other states:

> THE SUBJECTS OF THE GREAT MONARCH WHO OCCUPIES THE THRONE OF SPAIN SHOULD LEARN ONCE AND FOR ALL THAT THEY WERE BORN TO OBEY AND REMAIN SILENT AND NOT TO THINK OR GIVE THEIR OPINIONS ABOUT THE HIGH MATTERS OF GOVERNMENT.

Despite the efforts of the government and church, the ideas of the Enlightenment entered into select circles of men and women in New Spain. Banned books by Locke and Voltaire were secretly passed from person-to-person. In closed-door meetings the educated elite exchanged news about the country to the north, the United States, now thriving as a newly independent state. They also discussed events in Spain, whose government had been severely weakened by wars and upheavals led by European liberals.

In the early 1800s a book appeared in New Spain called *Periquillo Sarniento* ("Itching Parrot"). Written by José Joaquín Fernández de Lizardi, a *criollo* born in colonial Mexico, it became what many historians herald as the first great Spanish American novel. The story tells of a man who was born into minor wealth but possessed no unusual skills or talents. To avoid meaningful work, the man, whose nickname is the "Itching Parrot," became a minor official in village government. He is corrupt and harsh on the people under him. Itching Parrot is particularly brutal in his treatment of Indians: "Counter to all the royal orders protecting the Indians, we abused these unhappy people at our pleasure, making them work for us as much as we liked without paying them a centavo."

The novel *Itching Parrot* was a satire, a humorous attack on bad government within New Spain. Authorities discouraged people from reading the book, but it became a hit among the literate class. The story pointed out that the government of New Spain was inefficient and unfair to its people. Like the liberal literature circulating in Europe, the *Itching Parrot* planted a seed in the minds of the Mexican colonists: Now was the time for a change of government in New Spain.

Population figures of New Spain are sketchy. In 1808, the German scientist and geographer Alexander von Humboldt (1769-1859) traveled through the colony and estimated the population at 6.5 million. Of these people, fewer than 1 million were whites. Though they were a minority, the whites led New Spain's government and owned most of the land. The colony was in every respect a racial hierarchy where *gachupines* ruled.

Though whites were the privileged race, they did not speak with one voice. In colonial Mexico whites were divided into two distinct classes: the *criollos* and the *gachupines*. *Criollos* were whites born in New Spain. By 1800, some *criollo* whites could trace their family history back more than ten generations in Mexico. Such longstanding *criollos* no doubt had some Indian bloodlines, but they usually denied that part of their heritage. Although the *criollos* basked in comfort and money, they were intensely jealous of the power wielded by their rival class of whites, the *gachupines*. *Gachupines* (the word comes from spurs or horsemen) were whites born in Spain. Those Spanish-born whites enjoyed the trust of the mother country and held New Spain's highest government offices. *Gachupines* were also powerful officials in the church.

Gachupines formed an upper class within the upper class. In the early 1800s there were only a few thousand *gachupines*, compared to almost 1 million *criollos*. Still, the *gachupines* looked down on the native-born whites. *Gachupines* held a belief that life in the Americas made their fellow Europeans dull-witted and lazy. Worse yet, long association with the Americas divorced the *criollos* from Spain, thus diminishing their loyalties to the mother country. Recent developments in New Spain proved that this distrust of the *gachupines* about

Meaning of a Word

Early in the history of New Spain the word gachupin simply meant a white Spanish immigrant, and it was an accepted word with little negative connotation. As revolutionary fighting grew more bitter the word assumed a derisive character, becoming almost a swear word.

the *criollo*s was warranted: It was the *criollo*s who were more likely to utter the prohibited word—independence.

A rigid social ladder, based on racial definitions, governed every aspect of life in the colony. Spanish immigrants stood on the top step of the ladder. A step below the Spaniards were the *criollo*s, a comfortable but frustrated people. Below the *criollo*s were the mestizos, and below them the casts and the Indians. The government of Spain preserved this racial ladder because it helped to yoke the colony to the mother country. As long as the people of New Spain remained divided they could not act together and rebel against European authority.

A painting of the Virgin of Guadalupe atop a series of interracial couples with mixed-race children. *(Courtesy of Art Resources)*

Authorities feared that any change in the system would weaken the bond between Mexico and its European masters.

The mostly nonwhite lower classes knew little about the Enlightenment, the revolutions taking place in the outside world, and even about the rumblings for independence within New Spain itself. In fact, the nonwhites were hardly aware of rivalries between *criollos* and *gachupínes* because they saw all Spanish as owners or bosses. The whites were rich and they seemed to care little about the plight of the nonwhite masses. For Indians, mestizos, and casts, life was a constant struggle to give their families even food and a home. New Spain's economy centered on agriculture and mining, two enterprises owned almost exclusively by elite Spaniards. As a New Spain bishop wrote to the Spanish king, "All property and wealth is in Spanish hands. The Indians and the casts till the soil; they serve the upper class, and live only by the labor of their arms."

Since the Spanish conquest huge farms, called haciendas, were the rule in New Spain. Many haciendas spread out over tens of thousands of acres and they remained the same family's property for generations. Farmworkers were virtual slaves to the hacienda owner, usually a white *criollo*. If the owner wished, he could have a worker tied to the community whipping post and lashed to the point of death. Often the owner chose to live in the city, leaving the day-to-day hacienda operations to a foreman. The lives of the workers were governed by the overseer, and many of those men were known to be brutes.

Mine workers led even more dismal lives than farm peasants. Silver flowed from 5,000 Spanish-operated mines. By the early 1800s, New Spain produced more than one-fifth

Mexican silver mines produced much of the silver used to mint the widely circulated *ocho reales* (royal eights).

of the world's silver supply. The precious metal earned fortunes for a few whites, but it meant misery for thousands of mestizos and casts. Mine workers were sent, often naked, down ladders into the bowls of the earth where they hacked at the ground with picks and shovels in order to dig out the ore. Toiling in pitch blackness the workers waded in underground rivers with water up to their wastes. Rarely did a mine worker live beyond age forty. On the job, the miners breathed poisonous fumes and they were frequently killed by sudden explosions and cave-ins.

Mexican Silver

Spanish silver coins called *ocho reales* (royal eights) were a widely used currency throughout the world. The coins were made from silver mined in New Spain and Peru. Royal eights were also called "pieces of eight" and "Spanish dollars." Mexico remains a leading producer of silver to this day.

Impoverished people drowned their miseries in the powerful alcoholic drink pulque, a beer made from cactus. The government of New Spain had a monopoly on making or selling pulque and all other forms of alcoholic beverages. Alcohol was big business and its sale provided valuable tax revenues to the government. Crime rates soared as men and women sought money for their alcohol cravings. One Mexico City police official said, "Every pulque tavern is a forge of prostitution, robbery, homicide violent quarrels and all the other crimes that provide business for the courts. They are theaters where men and women are transformed into abominable hellish furies."

By 1810, dissatisfaction was everywhere. The government of New Spain treated the Indians as if they were children and the casts and mestizos as if they were drunkards and bandits. *Criollos* distrusted *gachupines* and *gachupines* condemned *criollos* as disloyal. Spain was in turmoil due to the forces of liberalism at loose on the European continent. For three hundred years Spain had ruled its prized colony of Mexico. Now the structure of New Spain stood as a house of cards set to blow apart with the slightest breeze.

FOUR

Hidalgo

Miguel Hidalgo y Costilla was born in central Mexico in 1753. He was a white *criollo* from a comfortable but not well-to-do family. His father was a hacienda overseer, one known to be fair to his workers. The elder Hidalgo preached the value of education to his family. As a boy, Miguel Hidalgo excelled in school and he devoured books. Philosophy was his passion. He read all the masters—Plato, Aristotle, and St. Augustine. He also read the enlightenment books which were banned by the government of New Spain. No law written could keep Hidalgo away from a book.

Hidalgo became a Catholic priest not so much because he felt an intense spiritual calling, but because the priesthood was a proper profession for a bright and learned young man. Being a priest allowed him to teach and share his love of books with others. Certainly Hidalgo was a devout Christian. He believed with all his heart in the glory of Christ and in the goodness of the church. However he was also a rebel, a rule breaker. Priests were supposed to deny themselves the love of a woman, yet Father Hidalgo had several girlfriends and it is believed he fathered at least three children. He enjoyed playing cards and dice games. Gambling debts disturbed his financial life and got him into trouble with high church officials.

Miguel Hidalgo y Costilla

As a young priest Hidalgo taught at San Nicolás, a Catholic college in Valladolid. In that college he met another priest, younger than him, named José María Morelos. Father Morelos would later loom as one of the great figures of Mexican independence. In 1803, Hidalgo was named parish priest in the town of Dolores in the state of Guanajuato. Guanajuato is north of Mexico City and is part of a broader region called the *Bajío* (lowland) that supports many large farms and silver mines. The city of Dolores had about 15,000 inhabitants when Father Hidalgo was assigned there; most of the townspeople were impoverished Indian farmworkers.

Tall, thin, and soft spoken, Father Hidalgo became loved by the people of Dolores. Growing up on his family's hacienda, he had learned Indian languages such as Otomi and Natahuatl, and he communicated in native speech with the farmworkers (campesinos). The Indian campesinos accepted him as a leader devoted to promoting their interests. Hidalgo was in his fifties, an old man by Mexican standards when he worked in Dolores. His parishioners believed his advanced years gave him great wisdom.

The beloved priest continued to break rules. By law Indians were forbidden to keep bees for the production of honey. This was one of a series of laws dating back to the conquest, and even Spanish judges could not explain the purpose of such rules. To Hidalgo, antiquated laws such as this were made to be broken. He wanted his parishioners to be economically independent and urged them to make and sell honey. He also assisted their efforts at wine-making and silk-weaving, two other fields closed by law to Indians. Government leaders complained about the activities of this rebel clergyman, but the town of Dolores was an isolated place. Father Hidalgo

Hidalgo taught the Indians of Dolores in an attempt to better their lives, although such teaching was often restricted by Spanish law.
(Courtesy of The Granger Collection)

continued teaching Indians useful trades despite the disapproval of church and government officials.

Meanwhile events in Spain grew confusing as the forces of liberalism plunged Europe into war and disorder. In 1808, the French army invaded Spain, conquered the country, and set up a French-dominated government. The Spaniards fought back. Militias in large Spanish towns such as Oviedo and Seville drove out French troops and declared themselves to be the true government of Spain. Because of the turmoil, no one could determine who really was in charge of Spanish affairs. These grave problems in the mother country triggered a debate on the other side of the world. People in Mexico asked why they should be ruled by a faraway European land that was itself in a state of chaos. *Criollo* and *gachupin* elite soundly rejected the legitimacy of the French ruler, planting the seed for discussions of either aggressive reform or complete independence.

Independence had long been a subject of secret discussions in New Spain, but only a few movements went beyond the talking stage. As early as 1565 native-born whites, including a son of Hernando Cortés, conspired in a plot to bring about Mexican independence. In 1650 an Irish-born immigrant named William Lamport wrote pamphlets in Mexico City urging the people to free themselves from the Spanish yoke. Spanish authorities ordered Lamport to be burned at the stake for the crime of treason.

Still, the idea of independence simmered in the minds of intellectual dreamers in New Spain. Early on these idealists made up no more than a handful of white *criollos*. Nonwhites were too impoverished and poorly educated to think beyond the day-to-day trials of providing food and shelter for their families. Many whites rejected independence because they lived as privileged citizens and wanted nothing to disturb their lofty status. Mindsets changed with the Enlightenment and the weakened government in Spain. Independence—though it was still a whispered word—became widely discussed.

In 1808, a Spanish sugar planter named Gabriel de Yermo organized an army of volunteers and managed to invade government offices and arrest the viceroy. Yermo represented the liberal factions in Spain, and he wanted to reduce the power

held by the *gachupínes* in colonial Mexico. The Yermo uprising was an attempt at government reform rather than a full
scale revolution aimed to bring about independence. Yermo
sought only a greater voice in government for native-born
criollos, and his efforts failed. Spanish authorities appointed
a new viceroy and the Mexican colony continued to be ruled
largely by the *gachupín* class.

In the Bajío region the move by Yermo intrigued independence-minded individuals. Yermo had, temporarily at least,
overthrown the government of New Spain and the authorities were too weak to punish him. The Bajío, more than one
hundred miles north of Mexico City, was frontier land, where
the people believed they were pioneers with little need to
obey laws issued from remote Mexico City.

In the heart of the Bajío lay the city of Querétaro, where the
Literary Club of Querétaro met with the announced purpose
of discussing books. In secret they took bold steps designed to

An eighteenth-century view of Querétaro, Mexico *(Library of Congress)*

bring about profound political change in the colony. The men and women of the club did not want to depose the Spanish king, nor were they enemies of the Catholic Church. Their primary aim was to reduce the power of the *gachupines* and allow native-born Mexicans to assume a responsible role in church matters and in government. Members of the Querétaro club envisioned a new government which would stand as an equal partner with the mother country. Ideally the club would create a state which would remain a member of the Spanish Empire under King Ferdinand VII, but enjoy home rule.

Members of the literary club included Miguel Domínguez, a high Querétaro official and his wife, Josefa Ortiz de Domínguez. The official had the title *Corregidor* and Josepha, his wife, is known in Mexican history as *La Corregidora*. Also in the club was Ignacio Allende from the nearby town of San Miguel El Grande (today called San Miguel de Allende). Allende was a wealthy *criollo* who served as an army officer over a militia unit. Another man associated with the club was Juan de Aldama, also from San Miguel El Grande.

The most radical club member was Father Miguel Hidalgo. Almost sixty, he was the oldest of the Querétaro conspirators. Father Hidalgo dreamed of a social revolution going well beyond the reform-minded aspirations of the others who wished mainly

Miguel Domínguez was a high Querétaro official and an active member of the Querétaro Literary Club.

to reduce *gachupín* power. Hidalgo hoped to liberate the nonwhites and make them equal citizens of a new society. Whites in the group were uneasy at the prospect of sharing power with nonwhites, but they needed the support of the mestizos and others if their movement were to succeed. High ranking members of the literary group asked Father Hidalgo to rally the nonwhites, and counted on his ability to control them. All knew that racial resentment brewed in New Spain. Whites feared that if authority broke down the nonwhite masses would take revenge on all white people—the *criollos* as well as the *gachupines.*

The Querétaro conspirators planned to announce their aims in December of 1810 at an annual fair held in the town of San Juan de Los Lagos north of Mexico City. Great crowds of people were expected to gather for the fair. The group hoped to broadcast their intentions to form a new government, rally the crowd to their cause, and march to Mexico City gathering supporters along the way. In case a fight broke out with Spanish authorities, Ignacio Allende and his militia army would be there at hand. In anticipation of possible battle, Father Hidalgo had secretly told his Indian supporters to make spears and sharpen machetes to be used as weapons. The priest prayed for peace, but he wanted his followers to be ready for any development.

As many as 3,000 people across the Bajío were privy to the revolutionary plans. With such a large number involved, the secret was bound to leak out to authorities. In one case several group members asked an army officer named Agustín de Iturbide to join their ranks. Iturbide had earlier displayed sympathy towards the idea of independence, but instead of joining the movement Iturbide reported the conspiracy

to Spanish officials. Ironically, Iturbide—the informant—
would later play a prominent role in the story of Mexican
independence. In another case of betrayal a group member
confessed his "sin" of plotting against the government to
a priest. The priest broke his solemn vows never to repeat
information gained during confession and divulged the
plans to police.

On September 13, 1810, key members of the literary group
were arrested in Querétaro. Josefa Ortiz de Domínguez, the
wife of the Corregidor, was ordered to be locked in her bed-
room for her part in the plan. Despite her confinement, she
managed to signal a sympathetic neighbor that the authorities
were aware of their plans. Within hours her warning reached
the town of Dolores and Father Hidalgo.

The Mexican historian Justo Sierra called Father Hidalgo,
"a man of ideas and action." Action was his highest calling.

Josefa Ortiz de Domínguez (1768–1829)

Known as *La Corregidora*, Josef Ortiz de Domínguez is today a
great heroine in Mexican history. She is hailed as the Paul Revere
of Mexico. La Corregidora risked her life and her freedom to
spread the warning of the impending arrests, and by doing so she
allowed the independence movement to continue. She paid for
her actions. Josefa Ortiz was forced to spend ten years in various
convents for the crime of conspiring against New Spain. Today a
handsome statue of her stands in Mexico City overlooking a plaza
which bears her name. Several Mexican schools are named after
the brave La Corregidora.

Knowing the group's carefully laid out plans had been exposed, Hidalgo decided to propel Mexico towards independence in the early morning hours of September 16, 1810. There was no time to wait. Gathering his most loyal followers, Hidalgo went to the city jail where he released the inmates and locked up Spaniards and others he suspected would be loyalists to New Spain. He then rang his church bell, and ushered in the most glorious moment in Mexican history.

Upon hearing the bell, Hidalgo's parishioners, most of them Indian and mestizo campesinos, gathered in the church-yard. Then, in the predawn darkness, Hidalgo delivered his famous *Grito de Dolores*.

The *Grito*

In towns and villages across Mexico, the night of September 15 is a very special night of the *Grito*. (The *Grito de Dolores* is also called the *Grito de Hidalgo*). At darkness, people gather in the town center. Finally, at eleven in the evening, the mayor or a special guest appears on a high balcony where he or she rings a bell. Then comes the *Grito*.

"Mexicanos, Viva Mexico!" (Mexicans, long live Mexico!), the speaker shouts.

"Viva!" answers the crowd.

"Viva la independencía" (Long live our independence)

"Viva!"

"Viva Hidalgo!"

"Viva!"

"Viva Allende!"

After several more "vivas" the speaker will cry out, "Viva Mexico!" At that moment a band bursts into the Mexican National Anthem and people in the crowd sing with the band as fireworks

---

explode in the night air. The next day, September 16, is officially Mexican Independence Day and it is celebrated with parades and patriotic speeches. Independence Day is a moving festival, but nothing equals the excitement of the *Grito*. Once every six years the president of Mexico travels to the town of Dolores Hidalgo. There the president stands on the church step, where Father Hidalgo once stood, and gives a very special version of the *Grito*.

That morning Father Miguel Hidalgo started a revolution. It was a completely spontaneous effort. The literary club had mapped out plans and specific goals for the movement to achieve, but the club had been broken up and many of its key members were now in jail. Because of the arrests the revolution began with no precise course of action or clear-cut objectives. Its warriors had only a few primitive weapons. Yet this rag-tag army had no shortage of courage. Excited by a spirit of freedom, the amateur soldiers were unafraid to fight or to die for a cause.

FIVE

The Battle of the Banners

Several thousand men and women set out led by Hidalgo, Allende, and Aldama. The revolutionary soldiers headed in the general direction of Guanajuato, the state capital. Their first stop was the small village of Atotonilco, where Hidalgo entered a church and removed a picture of the Virgin of Guadalupe from the wall. He attached the picture to a tall pole and joined his followers outside. Upon seeing the banner the revolutionaries fell to their knees, weeping and praying. The brown-skinned lady was revered especially by Mexico's nonwhites; Justo Sierra called the Virgin of Guadalupe, the "Indians' Mother of God."

Following the banner of Guadalupe, the army next marched to San Miguel, Ignacio Allende's birthplace. Here Allende commanded a battalion of professional soldiers who were well-armed and disciplined. Allende hoped his men would bring a degree of order to Hidalgo's followers, who were beginning to resemble a mob.

This mural by Juan O'Gorman shows Father Hidalgo leading the Mexican insurgents.
(Courtesy of The Granger Collection)

In San Miguel the rebels broke into shops and looted the homes of wealthy whites. It made no difference if the whites were sympathizers or enemies of independence. Whites represented money and power. Now, at last, the nonwhites were free to strike back at those who had long been their oppressors. As Justo Sierra wrote, "Liberty for [Hidalgo's followers] was not a right; it was an intoxication . . . an explosion of hate and joy."

Leadership of the revolt began to split. Allende wanted primarily to reduce the power of the *gachupines* and broaden the role *criollos* could play in government. Hidalgo aspired to a broader social revolution that would bring equality to all the races of Mexico. In San Miguel the mood of the revolutionary band turned ugly. The soldier Allende feared the revolutionary army, suddenly unshackled, was becoming drunk on its own powers. Hidalgo argued that Allende should overlook the pent-up passions released by the crowd. This occasion was, after all, the Mexican people's first taste of liberty. Both leaders were aware that the emotions generated by independence could unleash deep hatreds. The independence movement was, perhaps, on the brink of spiraling out of control and exploding into a race war.

From San Miguel the army marched again, this time toward the city of Celaya. On the road they looked more like a migrating hoard than an army. Women and children marched with the men, and many women held babies in their arms. The marchers were the poorest of the poor. Their clothes, little more than rags, hung to their bodies. Some soldiers of this amateur army were silver miners or farmworkers—young and fearless men who were itching for a fight. Gangs of professional bandits and roadside pirates freely joined the parade.

For weapons, the insurgents carried clubs, spears, and bows and arrows. Many had machetes, the long knives used by farmworkers to cut sugarcane and other crops. In the years to come the machete rose in status to become the sword of the revolution. Only a few of Hidalgo's men carried firearms, and the guns they bore were ancient.

As they traveled the rebels looted farms for corn and beans and killed cattle for meat. Since it was harvesttime the larger farms were well stocked with provisions. The stealing of food, of course, earned the resentment of local farmers who threatened to kill all looters. Ignacio Allende's disciplined soldiers rode on horseback trying to keep some degree of discipline.

At Celaya the insurgents broke into houses and churches searching for valuables. Some revolutionaries seized important Spaniards and held them for ransom. One group found a chest stuffed with silver coins, and with great roars of laughter threw the coins into the air and let them shower onto their heads. Once more Allende and Hidalgo argued over the raucous behavior of the crowd. Allende demanded order. Hidalgo counseled that a certain amount of wildness had to be tolerated among these people who had been near slaves for so many generations.

The insurgent ranks swelled to almost 50,000 as they made their way to the next goal: the city of Guanajuato. A rich silver mining center, Guanajuato was the jewel of the Bajío. Holding 66,000 residents, it was also the second-largest city in Mexico. Guanajuato contained marvelous churches and vine-covered houses owned by wealthy *gachupines* and *criollos.*

By this time the floodgates of hatred and rage were wide open in the Hidalgo-led force. The insurgents knew they were part of a movement designed to bring independence to Mexico, but independence was a vague word and held little meaning to people who had been hungry for most of their lives. The revolutionaries eyed gold and the goods owned by Spaniards. To them Guanajuato loomed as the ultimate prize.

Guanajuato was defended by José Antonio Riaño, an experienced officer in the Spanish army. He had few regular troops under his command, but his soldiers were loyal and determined to fight till death. Riaño ordered the wealthy white families to shelter in a thick-walled public grain storage building called the *Alhóndiga de Granaditas.* In proper military fashion, Riaño then organized his men in ranks in front of the granary building.

The insurgent army, proudly holding the banner of Guadalupe, reached the outskirts of Guanajuato on September 28, 1810. Father Hidalgo sent out emissaries asking Riaño to surrender the city. One of Hidalgo's officers read a letter aloud to the defenders. "I am at the head [of an army], and according to their will we wish independence of Spain and to govern ourselves. We have been in the tremendously humiliating and shameful position of 300 years of dependency under Spain, and the Spaniards' totally unjust profiteering from the wealth of Mexico."

General Riaño refused to surrender and the terrible Battle of Guanajuato broke out. For the first time the insurgents faced an organized army equipped with powerful weapons. Hidalgo's men charged into Spanish ranks shouting the battle cry, "Viva the Virgin of Guadalupe!" Riaño's soldiers cut the revolutionaries down with blasts from Spanish cannon. Again and again Hidalgo's soldiers attacked in reckless rushes, only to be slaughtered by cannon fire. Bodies piled up. Blood flowed in the streets.

Ignoring the carnage, the mass of attackers slowly gained the advantage. With courage recalling the Aztec warriors of old, the insurgents pressed close to the troops outside the granary and pelted them with stones and arrows. The soldiers were forced to retreat inside the Alhóndiga. Siege warfare thundered in Guanajuato. The Granary, with its strong stone walls, appeared to be impregnable. Spaniards inside the building had stored food and ammunition in sufficient quantities to hold out for many weeks. Raiño's soldiers positioned themselves on the Alhóndiga's ramparts and behind windows, and from these vantage points fired at the insurgents swarming on the streets below. Bodies of Hidalgo's men lay strewn outside the building. Wounded men, covered with blood, screamed as they struggled to crawl out of the line of fire.

A turning point in the battle came when one of Ignacio Allende's men shot and severely wounded commander Riaño.

The Alhondiga de Granaditas in Guanajuato *(Courtesy of Brian Atkinson/ Alamy)*

Spanish officers argued over who should take the commander's place. As the officers bickered a heroic act turned the sway of the fight towards the insurgents. A young mine worker, whose arms rippled with muscles, picked up a huge flagstone and held it above his head for protection against the bullets. The young man then raced to the wooden door of the granary and set it on fire with a torch. Hundreds of insurgents crashed through the weakened door and poured inside. Seventeen-year-old Lucas Alamán witnessed the storming of the building and later wrote, "[A Spanish officer] ordered his soldiers to fire at close range, and many of the assailants perished. Still, those in back of the crowd pushed forward, and the ones in front trampled over the dead, sweeping everything before them with an irresistible force."

The Alhóndiga became a scene of horror. Spaniards tried to surrender but were clubbed to death by the insurgents. Some Spaniards stood on upper balconies and threw down gold and silver coins hoping to be spared. Others dropped to their knees and begged for their lives. Few escaped death. The battle became a massacre. The insurgents cared little if the victims were *criollo* or *gachupin*. All were rich. All were white. All were enemies.

"El Pípila"

The silver miner who set fire to the granary door was José de los Reyes Martínez, who is today a hero in Mexican history. Martínez is known by his nickname, "*El Pípila*," a word for turtle. The nickname comes from the fact that he held a large stone over his back and head, like a turtle's shell, when he set fire to the Alhóndiga door. A colossal statue of El Pípila holding a flaming torch now stands on a hill in Guanajuato not far from the Alhóndiga. Erected in 1939, the statue is a major tourist attraction.

The capture of the granary building led to a spree of looting and violence which spread throughout the city. The young Lucas Alamán reported, "The insurgents, after taking over the Alhóndiga, gave free reign to their vengefulness . . . many young men of the city's most distinguished families died. Those who remained alive—naked, covered with wounds, tied up with rope—were taken to the public jail."

Rioting raged for two days as hatred gripped Hidalgo's followers. About five hundred Guanajuato residents were killed by marauding mobs. During the battle for the city almost 2,000 insurgents lost their lives. Surviving citizens of Guanajuato were left dazed as they surveyed the ruins of their city.

Militarily, Guanajuato was a victory for Hidalgo, but the naked violence displayed by his army set back the cause of independence. Whites in New Spain had long feared an uprising by nonwhites. In Guanajuato the dreaded racial war had taken place and resulted in terrible bloodletting. *Criollos* now united with *gachupínes* as both felt an urgent need to stamp out the dark-skinned insurgent army. Independence, the heartfelt desire of many *criollos*, would simply have to wait for a more opportune moment. All whites feared for their lives.

Campaigns of Hidalgo

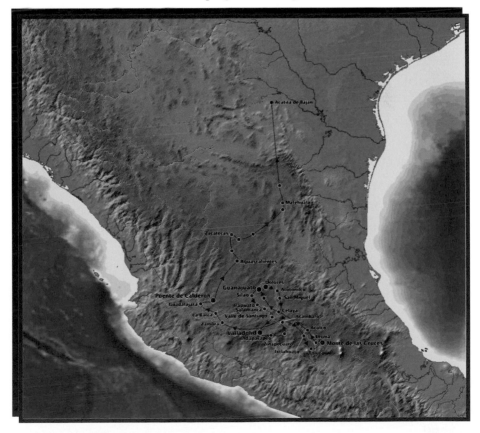

From Guanajuato the insurgents marched to the city of Valladolid, where Hidalgo had once taught at the university. His army now numbered thousands of peasants, all of whom were willing to fight and kill. Valladolid city leaders surrendered and thereby escaped the slaughter that befell Guanajuato. The ranking Catholic bishop in the city officially excommunicated Hidalgo (ousted him from the Catholic Church) for his role in heading the insurgents. Excommunication hurt him deeply as Hidalgo had dedicated his life to the church. He said of the church and the foes of independence, "I am a true Catholic. Our enemies are Catholics only out of politics. Their God is money."

By the end of October the insurgent army, now 80,000 strong, trekked toward Mexico City. This force, still flying the banner of Guadalupe, was the largest army seen in Mexico since the fall of the Aztec Empire. Hidalgo was at this point as much a follower as he was a leader of the army. The revolution now possessed a spirit of its own, flowing in directions Hidalgo could not control. The flame was lit and the desire for independence stirred up revolts in northern and southern Mexico. As historian Justo Sierra wrote, "In any case the movement had caught on. Armed bands rose in revolt everywhere."

Mexico City was defended by a Spanish general named Trujillo, who commanded about 7,000 troops. General Trujillo made a stand at a mountain pass outside the capital called *Monte de las Cruces* (Mountain of the Crosses), so named because here roadside bandits were crucified as punishment.

Though he was vastly outnumbered, Trujillo had cannons and employed them skillfully. The battle began with Hidalgo's men charging into the face of the artillery blasts while shouting, "Viva the Virgin of Guadalupe!" Fire from the cannons slaughtered the insurgents by the hundreds. When they finally closed in on the big guns, some of the Indian warriors held their straw hats over the muzzles believing this action would silence the thundering beasts. The fight for Monte de las Cruces lasted the entire day of October 30, 1810. An estimated 2,000 insurgents were killed, but the rebels forced General Trujillo to retreat.

Mexico City now lay open and defenseless. City residents, especially the rich whites, feared another Guanajuato on an even larger scale. The capital's citizens flocked to the churches and prayed with every passion in their hearts for God to come to Earth and drive the rebel army from the city gates.

Viceroy Francisco Venegas ordered the little wooden doll called the Virgin of los Remedios to be put on a wagon and paraded through the streets. Three hundred years earlier Spanish conquistadors carried this image of los Remedios into battle when they conquered the Aztecs. The doll was now viewed as a sacred relic representing Spain's power in the Mexican colony. The viceroy took the tiny statute to the city's Cathedral and with tears streaming down his face proclaimed it to be the commanding general of Spanish forces defending Mexico City. The Virgin of Los Remedios was painted white, in sharp contrast with the brown-skinned Virgin of Guadalupe. So a symbolic clash of holy women, a battle of the banners, loomed. It was as if the saints themselves had chosen sides in the coming fight for Mexico City.

After assembling his forces outside the city, Hidalgo suddenly called off the attack. The battle that pitted the Virgin of Guadalupe against the Virgin of Los Remedios was never fought.

Historians still argue why Hidalgo cancelled the march on Mexico City. A huge Spanish army coming to reinforce the capital was near. Perhaps Hidalgo feared the consequences of going against such a large and organized group of soldiers. Also Allende's troops had little ammunition for their firearms, and there were few sympathetic *criollos* willing to resupply them. Finally, many historians conclude, Hidalgo was struck with pangs of conscience. He was at heart a gentle soul who abhorred violence. The priest worried that his angry followers would bring a bloodbath to Mexico City. Rather than foster more violence, Hidalgo called off the attack.

The retreat outside of Mexico City turned the tide for Hidalgo and his independence movement. The passion of the *Grito* and the energy generated by the banner of the Virgin of Guadalupe drained away. Revolutionaries feared the movement had died, and many of his followers had to return to their crops and businesses.

Hidalgo set up a rival government in the city of Guadalajara. He appointed ministers and printed an official government-sponsored newspaper. Few paid heed to Hidalgo's self-proclaimed government. Powerful *criollos* within Guadalajara were openly hostile to the rebel priest.

Ignacio Allende traveled north hoping to gain assistance from the United States. Allende knew that the Americans coveted Texas, which was then part of New Spain's northern frontier. Ignacio Allende hoped a deal could be worked out and his forces could gain fresh arms and supplies in exchange for surrendering regions of Texas' territory.

Meanwhile Viceroy Venegas promoted a Spanish army officer, Félix María Calleja, to the rank of general. Calleja proved to be a brutal but effective commander. General Calleja

Félix Maria Calleja's methods of quelling the insurgents' revolt were brutal but effective. *(Courtesy of The Granger Collection)*

reoccupied the city of Guanajuato, where he proceeded to hang all mestizos and casts whom he suspected of fighting on Hidalgo's side. Under Calleja the revolutionary war drifted into a particularly cruel stage. Both sides engaged in torture and in ghastly executions such as burning captured soldiers alive.

In January 1811, Hidalgo's forces met Calleja's army at the bridge of Calderón near Guadalajara. Calleja's soldiers were outnumbered nearly ten to one, but they had the advantage of superior weapons and military discipline. The insurgents fought with their customary courage, charging the enemy amid cries of "Viva the Virgin of Guadalupe!" But a random event swung the fortunes of battle in favor of the Spaniards. A cannon shell hit an insurgent horse-drawn wagon carrying gunpowder, and a tremendous explosion ripped the battlefield. The blast left Hidalgo's men stunned and shocked. Some thought the fires of hell had gushed forth from the bowels of the earth and struck their ranks. Hidalgo's soldiers broke and ran.

The independence movement, as led by Father Hidalgo, disappeared in the smoke rising at the Battle of Calderón. Never again would Hidalgo raise a large army and lead it into battle. Allende still hoped to find help in the United States, but he was captured by Spanish forces long before he reached his goal. Juan de Aldama and another rebel officer, Domingo Jiménez, were also caught. Father Miguel Hidalgo was arrested and thrown into a jail cell on March 21, 1811, barely six months after he electrified Mexico with the *Grito* that sent the colony storming towards independence.

Beginning in May 1811, military trials were held for Allende, Aldama, and Jiménez. All three men were found guilty and shot by firing squads. Hidalgo was a special case. He was still a priest even though one bishop had excommunicated him. Spanish law forbade priests to be tried by a military court. Hidalgo faced a church court where he refused to ask for a pardon; "pardon is for criminals, not for defenders of the country," he said. The court found him guilty.

On the morning of July 30, 1811, Father Hidalgo faced a firing squad. Forgiving to the end, the priest stood before the soldiers quietly accepting death. An officer claimed Hidalgo, "stared straight at us with those beautiful eyes."

In the months to come the heads of Hidalgo, Allende, Aldama, and Jiménez were cut off and shipped to Guanajuato.

There the heads were displayed in cagelike devices on each corner of the granary, the scene of the great Spanish slaughter. The heads hung suspended from that building for the next ten years. To this day the names of each martyr of the revolt are carved near the roof of the Alhóndiga to indicate where the head once was situated. Spanish authorities determined that these heads on display, with their eyes staring into eternity, would dash the hopes of future insurgents who dreamed of independence.

But the fire of independence was lit with the *Grito de Dolores* and no Spanish threats or brutal punishments could quench the flames.

SIX

Guerilla Warfare

After the executions of Hidalgo and Allende, leadership of the revolution passed at first to Ignacio López Rayón, a lawyer born in the state of Michoacán. He had been a close associate of Father Hidalgo, and he had acted as secretary of state for the revolutionary government Hidalgo had established in Guadalajara. Rayón moved into the mountain town of Zitácuar in southern Mexico and fortified the village with a moat and high walls to fend off Spanish attacks.

From his fortress town Rayón operated a rival government. He issued laws and printed communiqués on a printing press that was once the property of the Spain. The rival government minted copper coins and asked Mexicans to use them as currency until independence was achieved, and then the copper would be exchanged with silver. Rayón preserved the original aims of the independence movement, believing Mexico should reduce the power of the *gachupínes*, but stay

Ignacio López Rayón began leading the revolution after the executions of Hidalgo and Allende. *(Courtesy of The Granger Collection)*

within the broader Spanish Empire. Ignacio López Rayón insisted he was not an enemy of the king of Spain.

Supporting Rayón and his independence movement was a secret society in Mexico City called the Guadalupes. The society was made up largely of businessmen who silently worked towards independence, but maintained their jobs and businesses as they had in the past. The Guadalupes contributed money to the cause, and called themselves the Guadalupes to display their attachment to the Virgin of Guadalupe. Throughout the Mexican War of Independence, the Virgin of Guadalupe reigned as the symbol of the revolutionaries.

Many well-to-do *criollos* backed Rayón and flocked to his Zitácuar stronghold. One independence-minded man was a doctor named José María Cos, who served as the intellectual arm of the cause. Another *criollo*, the poet Andrés Quintana Roo, went to Zitácuar where he poured his energy into writing pamphlets and became a leading spokesman for the movement.

The young poet, Quintana Roo, had a girlfriend named Leona Vicario. Their relationship blossomed into a great love story of Mexican indepen-dence. Leona Vicario was an upper-class *criollo* who grew up in Mexico City. Her life was one of pampering and privileges, visiting the city's best shops during the day and attending the theater at night, always accompanied by a chaperon. Leona Vicario's family was conservative and pro-Spanish; her father was a *gachupín*. Despite her wealth and her Spanish ties, she caught the spirit of the revolution. When Hidalgo and his army were poised outside the capital the young

Andrés Quintana Roo became a leading spokesman for the independence movement. *(Courtesy of The Granger Collection)*

Leona Vicario *(Courtesy of The Granger Collection)*

Leona Vicario stood on her balcony shouting, "Long live my brothers the insurgents."

This radical behavior shocked Leona Vicario's conservative family. Her uncle, who was her official guardian, had her incarcerated in a woman's convent that was notorious for its strict rules. Leona was rescued from convent by a rebel band; she joined Quintana Roo in Zitácuar where the two married. Working together, the couple published fiercely worded pamphlets which urged Mexicans to continue marching on the path toward independence.

In those days soldiering was strictly a man's job, but Leona Vicario inspired women to contribute to the cause. Independence-minded women smuggled food to the insurgents and hid weapons under their broad skirts. Leona and her husband remained heroes of independence until their deaths. The couple now lies buried side by side under the landmark Column of Independence in Mexico City.

López Rayón and his associates at Zitácuar carried on the intellectual activity of the independence movement. Working as a second government, they passed laws and appointed high officers. But in the countryside, especially in the south of Mexico, a different fire burned. New and more radical leaders emerged, with their own ideas for winning independence.

After Hidalgo's defeat it was clear that Spanish authorities would fight to hold their prized colony. Ragtag revolutionary bands stood little chance of success in open battle against organized Spanish armies. So the rebels of New Spain imitated their contemporaries in Spain by fighting little wars—*guerilla wars*—against their oppressors. The new insurgents occupied the farms and small villages. Their soldiers were tough Indian and mestizo farmers who were rugged horsemen and knew the lay of the land. Small groups of these rebels raided Spanish-run towns and attacked supply columns. Frustrated Spanish army leaders could not stop the raids. Guerilla fighters seemed to drop from the sky during the day and disappear underground at nightfall.

There was no central authority, no Hidalgo-type leader in the guerilla warfare phase. Each region spawned a chieftain who rose to become a master of his territory. With no national leaders or overall goals, confusion and lawlessness gripped the independence movement. Some military strongmen were

Guerilla Warfare

Beginning in 1808 the armies of France occupied large parts of Spain. Spanish patriots who fought the French employed hit-and-run tactics to win minor skirmishes in their country. In Spanish the word for war is *guerra,* and the anti-French forces used the term *guerilla* (little war) to describe their operations. The pronunciation of the Spanish word for little wars is gurr-ee-aa, but in English it usually comes out gorilla, like the animal. The word has endured through the years. To this day when a small country wages limited battles to frustrate an occupying army, they are said to be engaging in guerilla warfare.

mere bandits who used the cause of independence as an excuse to rob and plunder. The chieftains even fought each other over the boundaries of their self-proclaimed territories. To many Mexicans who yearned with all their hearts to gain independence, the guerilla warfare raging in the countryside was deeply disheartening. Men and women learned to fear the guerilla chiefs more than they did Spanish authorities.

Yet several genuine heroes of Mexican independence rose from the bloody guerilla warfare sweeping the country. These local leaders were a different lot from Hidalgo and Allende, who were white and educated. The new leaders came from humbler origins. Often the guerilla chiefs were mestizos, and many could not read or write.

One such guerilla leader was Vicente Guerrero, an uneducated man of Spanish, Indian, and African bloodlines. Utterly devoted to the cause of independence, Guerrero commanded fierce loyalties among his followers. Living off the land in the mountains and forests of southern Mexico, Guerrero led an army of about 2,000 insurgents. Their weapons consisted largely of axes, clubs, and machetes. What they lacked in equipment they made up with aggressiveness. Guerrero's peasant army harassed the Spaniards with hit-and-run raids. Vicente Guerrero personally commanded almost all the operations. A skilled tactician he knew every twist in the mountain trails. In battle Guerrero inflicted far more casualties on enemy forces than he suffered.

State Names

Officially, modern Mexico is called *Estados Unidos Mexicanos* (United Mexican States). Like its neighbor to the north the country is made up of states, all of which have a capital city and a degree of home rule. Present-day Mexico has thirty-one states and one federal district. Most Mexican state names are Indian in origin, but four states—Guerrero, Hidalgo, Morelos, and Quintana Roo—are named for heroes in the independence movement.

Another guerilla leader was Albino García, a mestizo from the state of Guanajuato. A superb rider himself, García developed an ingenious technique to defeat enemy cavalrymen. In battle he sent two lines of his men riding in a close side-by-side formation toward an enemy unit of horse soldiers. At the last moment García ordered the two lines to split, revealing ropes tied between their saddles. The taught ropes then swept the opponents off their horses. García was fearless and acted as a true rebel who followed no one's orders. He once said he recognized no "highness" but the hills.

To counter the guerilla revolts, Spain turned to its most able and also its cruelest general: Félix María Calleja. The general's tactics brought a reign of terror to colonial Mexico. Any village even suspected of supporting the guerillas was burned and their residents slaughtered. Calleja's own soldiers feared him as the general was quick to order execution by firing squad for any man who disobeyed even the slightest of army rules. It was said that even the viceroy in Mexico City appeared uncomfortable in Calleja's presence.

At first it seemed that Calleja's barbaric tactics would succeed. Guerilla warfare dwindled, and by the end of 1811 some observers said the Mexican War of Independence was all but over. However one man, through courage and stubborn determination, kept the torch aflame. He was José María Morelos. Aside from Hidalgo, Morelos was the most important figure in the cause that finally gave Mexico freedom from Spanish rule.

SEVEN
Morelos

J osé María Morelos y Pavón was born in 1765 in the Mexican state of Michoacán. He was a dark-skinned mestizo who probably had African blood. Some historians claim Morelos should have been properly categorized as a *casta* by New Spain's color-conscious legal system. Morelos's father was a carpenter who was frequently unemployed. The family lived in poverty on a small farm owned by an uncle.

With the encouragement of his mother (she was the daughter of a school teacher) Morelos learned to read. He devoured books, reading by candlelight endless hours in the evenings. Also through his mother he mastered Spanish grammar and became an excellent writer.

In his youth Morelos worked as a mule driver on the "China Road," a mountain trail linking the Pacific port of Acapulco to Mexico City. The trail was called the China Road because it brought spices, silk, and other expensive

José María Morelos y Pavón *(Courtesy of The Granger Collection)*

goods from the Orient to New Spain's capital. The job as mule driver brought the young Morelos adventure, and it no doubt cultivated within him a taste for danger because the China Road was ridden with bandits. But mule-driving was not a fitting job occupation for a bookish man such as Morelos who yearned for scholarship.

When he was twenty-five Morelos enrolled in school to study for the priesthood. His decision to become a priest was similar to that made by Hidalgo. He believed the priesthood was a proper profession for an intellectual youth in

New Spain. Being a priest meant he could study, learn, and bring the joy of books to others. Also, again like Hidalgo, the young Morelos was certain the Catholic Church offered hope to the world. Morelos saw the glory of God everywhere. He longed to bring the Christian gospel to others, especially to the poor and nonwhite classes of New Spain.

The first church school Morelos attended was San Nicolás Obispo College in the city of Valladolid, about 130 miles west of Mexico City. The rector of that college was Father Miguel Hidalgo. Morelos studied under the future independence leader, but it is unknown how close the two were. Morelos later attended the Royal University in Mexico City.

Upon becoming a priest Morelos was assigned to a small parish in Michoacán. This was the tierra caliente (hot lands), a region of disagreeable weather where impoverished Indians lived. Morelos complained the assignment brought him, "bad weather and little profit."

With great energy Morelos served the people of the hot lands of southern Mexico. He inherited carpenter skills from his father and took great pride in a church he built largely with his own hands, later calling it "the best [church] in the tierra caliente." Unlike Hidalgo, Morelos was not a gentle priest cherished by all members of his flock. "He yells at us and he makes us angry and he treats us badly," his parishioners complained in a formal letter. Nor did Morelos always hold high esteem for the men and women attending his masses; he once said, "they are very much vagabonds."

Still, the people of southern Mexico applauded the young priest for his dedication. Morelos was demanding when leading his parishioners towards a proper Christian life, but he also sacrificed his comforts and sometimes his safety by traveling to remote villages and entering the shabby huts to minister to the sick and dying. "I am a miserable man, more so than most," Father Morelos once wrote, "and my nature is to be of service to an honest man, to lift him up when he has fallen, to pay his bills when he has no money and to offer whatever manner of assistance I can to someone in need, whoever that may be."

For almost twenty years Father Morelos worked as a faithful priest to the impoverished people of the tierra caliente. No promotions to higher offices within the church were offered to this humble priest. Morelos accepted his status without complaint because he was content to devote his life to uplifting his mostly Indian parishioners. Like Hidalgo, he urged his people to strive for financial independence by opening small businesses. He sometimes took money he earned from his own tiny salary and loaned it to an enterprising young person who wanted to start a small store or shop. Also like Hidalgo, he disobeyed his priestly vow of celibacy. Morelos lived with women, and it is believed he fathered three children.

The Catholic Church remained the focus of Morelos's life. As a voracious reader, Morelos studied the ideas of the Enlightenment. He agreed with most of the tenants of liberalism but took exception on the subject of religion. European liberals believed that countries ought to pass laws guaranteeing citizens freedom of religion. Morelos disagreed. Catholicism was the state religion in both Spain and New Spain, and Father Morelos wanted it to stay that way. In the early 1800s, Morelos wrote that he was, "totally ready to sacrifice my life for the Catholic religion."

Above all, Morelos hated injustice. He saw in New Spain a country where laws stripped Indians and other nonwhites of their rights as citizens. In a letter he once said the color of one's skin does not, "change one's heart or one's way of thinking." Morelos's nation also fostered a woefully unequal economic system. Select families (mostly whites) owned land which stretched to the horizon while the masses (nonwhites) were virtually landless. Morelos told the Spaniards that they must give "our campesinos the fruits of their labors;" farmland, he said, rightfully belonged to those "who tilled it."

Morelos came to believe only a successful revolution and independence from Spain could bring about the reforms his society desperately needed. He wrote, "[We must] overthrow all tyranny, substituting liberalism, and remove from our soil the Spanish enemy that has so forcefully declared itself against the Nation."

In 1810, Morelos met with his old professor, Father Hidalgo, at the town of Valladolid. At the time most of Mexico was aflame with revolutionary war. Morelos offered his services to the cause and asked to be an army chaplain for the insurgents. Hidalgo saw a higher calling for his one-time student, recognizing Morelos as a potential leader who could command the respect of others, especially the impoverished Indians. Father Hidalgo asked Morelos to raise an army and command it in southern Mexico.

At the time of his meeting with Hidalgo, Morelos was forty-five years old. He had no experience as a military leader, and he certainly did not look like an army commander. Morelos was barely five feet tall and was given to have a potbelly. He was frequently ill and bedeviled by almost constant headaches. But Morelos believed with all his heart in the cause of Mexican freedom and had tremendous respect for Father Hidalgo. Despite his misgivings—he had no idea if he could succeed as military commander—Morelos agreed to lead an army. With Father Morelos now devoted to the cause, a new chapter in the Mexican War of Independence began.

Morelos' first assignment as an insurgent chief was to seize the port city of Acapulco. The harbor on the Pacific was important to the Spanish royalists because it received luxury goods from Asia, thus allowing the national government to collect taxes on the imported items. Stripping the royalists of Acapulco's tax revenue would hurt their war effort.

Morelos set off to Acapulco, gathering an army as he traveled. After spending many years as a preacher he knew how to command attention. In the villages he explained the need for Mexican independence and asked for volunteer soldiers. The men he accepted into his army were mostly Indians and *castas*—rugged young men who had lived in poverty and were accustomed to hardships. Having few weapons, he had to turn down more volunteers than he accepted. When he finally arrived at the outskirts of Acapulco he commanded only a few dozen soldiers.

Morelos sent parties ahead to scout out Acapulco's defenses. The advance parties reported the city was protected by cannon and high walls, but it had few regular soldiers. Morelos decided to attack. His assault failed miserably as the men were cut down by the well-trained guard units. Morelos called off the offensive and his forces melted into the mountains and forests outside of town.

Even in defeat Morelos displayed his budding military ability. A lesser commander would have pressed home the assault on Acapulco, ignoring the loss of his soldiers. Morelos decided to wait and build up his forces so that he could continue the offensive later on more favorable terms. Meanwhile his men staged a guerilla war in the mountains surrounding the town. This was the region of the China Road where Morelos had worked as a mule driver when he was young. He knew the ebbs and flows of this land and used his knowledge wisely. Every twist in the road, every patch of forest became a hiding place for his guerilla soldiers. Morelos did not occupy Acapulco, but he isolated the city cutting off its resources from the royalists.

Morelos was, nominally at least, under the command of Ignacio López Rayón who governed from his headquarters at Zitácuar. Father Morelos happily accepted this arrangement. He believed that burning ambition destroyed men, and he had no desire to assume a high position in the insurgency. However he discovered that Rayón and the other officers at Zitácuar were indecisive and too given to refer decision-making to bulky committees. Most of the Zitácuar leaders were lawyers by trade and tended to argue every detail before they acted. Morelos, though, was in the field fighting Spaniards, and his decisions had to come fast. So, for the most part, Morelos acted alone and without counsel from superiors. Whether he wished to or not he rose to become the most important insurgent commander in southern Mexico.

Procuring weapons was a prime object of Morelos's raids. Each successful attack on a small Spanish army unit netted rifles and perhaps a light artillery piece. Many of Morelos's men had never seen a rifle much less fired one. Between battles Morelos drilled his troops and had them practice rifle skills. Here the commander's reading habits paid off. Morelos read any book that dropped into his hands, including a work called

Military Instructions written by Frederick the Great, King of Prussia. Frederick the Great molded the Prussian army into the strongest force in Europe by thoroughly training his soldiers and expecting obedience from them at all times. Father Morelos became Frederick's student from afar. In the mountains and deep valleys of southern Mexico he built the finest army of the insurgency.

Volunteers hastened to join Morelos's army in the south. Morelos accepted new men in numbers lim-

Morelos trained his soldiers using techniques he learned from studying the work of Frederick the Great (above).

ited only by his cache of weapons. Unlike Hidalgo, Morelos refused to send men into battle armed only with clubs and machetes. "Entire villages keep wanting to follow me, eager to be with me in the fight for independence," he wrote, "but I prevent them from doing so, telling them that their help would be much more powerful through working the land to supply food for us who launch ourselves into war."

Morelos became a far more successful military leader than Hidalgo. He possessed a natural gift for military tactics. After just one look at a stretch of land he automatically determined the best spot to launch an attack or the most advantageous place to wage a defensive battle. Always he relied on the element of surprise to achieve victory. In battle his personal courage inspired the men under him. A historian who observed him in combat described his leadership under fire as, "calm, without excitement, without hotheadedness."

Morelos also had a talent for appointing outstanding officers. The superb guerilla leader Vicente Guerrero remained one of his leading sub commanders. Allied with Guerrero was a wealthy *criollo* named Nicolás Bravo, who would later take a high position in Mexican government. Mariano Matamoros, a priest who shared Morelos's strong views on religion, was another excellent field leader in his army. Morelos was so close with Mariano Matamoros that he once called him his, "good right arm." A favorite officer was Félix Fernández, who later changed his name to Guadalupe Victoria, to honor Mexico's special saint and Victoria for "victory." The Virgin of Guadalupe remained sacred to all of Father Morelos's soldiers.

As they acquired more weapons the insurgent army of Morelos grew. By the end of 1811 he commanded 9,000 well-trained and reasonably well-equipped soldiers. The Morelos force controlled a vast territory stretching from the outskirts of Acapulco north and east almost to Mexico City. The presence of this rebel army in the south infuriated New Spain's leaders, especially General Félix María Calleja. The general set out to rectify the perilous situation and deal with the upstart Father Morelos.

Nicolás Bravo served as one of Morelos's high-ranking officers.
(Courtesy of the New York Public Library)

General Calleja marched first to Zitácuaro, the headquarters of López Rayón. He was the man operating the rival government and was, it appeared to outsiders, giving Morelos his orders. Calleja sacked and burned the fortified town of Zitácuaro. Rayón abandoned his stronghold and escaped into the hills when he first heard word of the approaching army. This act of flight saved Rayón's life but forfeited his influence over the insurgent government, leaving Morelos alone to keep the hopes of Mexican independence alive.

In February 1812, Calleja led his forces into the state of Michoacán in the heart of Morelos-controlled territory. Father Morelos was too smart a military leader to engage this powerful army in an open field. Instead he and 3,000 of his best troops waited for Calleja in the hill town of Cuautla. Morelos hoped to lure his foe into the town and force him to fight a house-by-house and street-by-street battle. Guerilla fighters were especially effective when waging such warfare and Morelos believed the townspeople would join his side against the hated Spaniards.

Calleja, also a clever general, refused to take the bait offered by his rival. Upon arriving at Cuautla he ordered his troops to surround the town and lay siege to it. An agonizing but storied chapter in Mexican history was written at Cuautla. Calleja's artillery blasted the town. Children defied the cannon fire, gathering the spent balls, and gave them to Morelos' gunners. With the town surrounded, supplies became exhausted. Townspeople as well as Morelos's men were reduced to eating rats and tree bark. Still no one gave thought to surrender. Mexican history books today talk in glorious terms of the defenders of Cuautla who resisted the Spaniards despite their own desperate circumstance.

Morelos formulated a plan to break out of the besieged town. The spring rainy season would soon begin. Calleja's soldiers were mostly from northern climates and Morelos reasoned they would be unable to deal with the soggy heat of the *tierra caliente* during rainy season. Morelos hoped unfavorable weather would force the Spaniards to withdraw. However even nature conspired against the insurgents. The time for the usual spring rains came and went, and day after day the skies were cloudless.

On May 2, 1812, with Spanish soldiers still surrounding the town, Morelos attempted to escape Cuautla with his troops. He waited till nightfall hoping to catch the Spaniards by surprise. Most of the townspeople prepared to evacuate with the army because they feared General Calleja's wrath when he stormed into their city.

The mass retreat began well, but noise soon alerted Spanish sentries. Shots and wild yells rang out in the night. Morelos was prepared for this possibility. Before setting out he had divided his men into small groups, each group commanded by a trusted sergeant. He instructed the sergeants

to avoid firefights with the Spaniards and instead lead their units out of town. Later the groups would gather at a rallying point. The sergeants carried out their duties expertly. Most of the men and the townspeople escaped.

This painting depicts Morelos's nighttime escape from the besieged town of Cuautla. *(Courtesy of Look and Learn Magazine, Ltd./The Bridgeman Art Library)*

The next day Calleja marched into the city to find it inhabited only by a few women, children, and some old people who were too sick or too weak from hunger to move out with Morelos. The general slaughtered them all. Calleja then returned to Mexico City claiming he had scored a stunning victory over Morelos and his band of rebels holed up at Cuautla.

The Mexico City public doubted General Calleja's claim of victory. A hastily written play appeared at Mexico City theaters. The drama harkened back to the time when the Moors occupied Spain. A Spanish general, returning from battle, claims victory over the Moors and presents his king with a cloth turban which he claims to have taken from the enemy commander. The king asks what became of the Moor. Sheepishly the general admits his enemy escaped. Theatergoers roared with laughter at the plight of this hapless general. All knew the true message of the play. The leader of Mexican independence—Father José María Morelos y Pavón—was at-large and ready to continue the fight despite General Calleja's boastful claims of victory.

EIGHT

The Dream and the Defeat

B y early summer 1812, Morelos had regrouped his army and expanded his territory in the south. He quickly reoccupied Cuautla and overwhelmed Oaxaca, thoroughly defeating the Spanish defenders there. Near Veracruz his men burnt tobacco fields, depriving the government a wealth of tax revenue. In the spring of 1813 Morelos took Acapulco, his original goal. Now all of southern Mexico was firmly under the control of the insurgent priest.

Some of Morelos's advisers urged him to march on Mexico City. The army of the south had grown to as many as 15,000 members and was perhaps strong enough to conquer the capital. However Morelos preferred to isolate Mexico City and build up his strength in the countryside. Operating in the rural regions, Morelos controlled the roads leading from the capital to both the Atlantic and the Pacific coasts. The Spanish regime in Mexico City, cut off from trade and communications, weakened.

In 1813, Morelos formally declared Mexican independence and began work on establishing a new country. He named the country the Republic of Anáhuac, after an ancient name for the Valley of Mexico which embraced Mexico City. The nation was to be a republic, with no king or queen. Here Morelos differed from earlier revolutionaries who wanted to preserve the Spanish monarchy but reduce the power of the *gachupínes.*

Establishing a new government with a constitution based on laws had long been Morelos's goal. Morelos was a remarkably humble man who shunned personal glories. He desired no office in the government he was creating. Nor did he enjoy his role as a military commander. Once a republican form of government was established and in operation, he hoped to return to life as a parish priest. He said the only title he desired was that of "servant of the people."

Morelos assembled a congress at the town of Chilpancingo for the purpose of writing a constitution to be used by the republic. The congressmen charged with writing the document were mainly *criollo* lawyers and priests. With Morelos providing leadership, the constitution they produced was a manifesto of liberalism. First the constitution reaffirmed independence: "That America is free and independent of Spain and all other Nations, Governments, or Monarchies." The document also established a democracy with a representative form of government: "That sovereignty springs directly from the People . . . whose powers shall be divided into Legislative, Executive, and Judiciary branches, with each Province electing its representative."

Language in the constitution wiped out the social status based on skin color that had plagued New Spain. All citizens

Morelos wanted Catholicism to remain the only religion allowed in Mexico. Shown here is an 1899 photo of the Cathedral of Mexico. *(Library of Congress)*

of the Republic of Anáhuac were to enjoy equality under the law. Morelos wanted to go further still and address the problem of unequal land ownership. The priest urged the lawmakers to write legislation breaking up all haciendas larger that six square miles and giving the excess land to the peasants. To Morelos's disappointment, terms calling for land reform did not appear in the final document.

In matters of religion, Morelos departed with liberalism as it was advocated by European intellectuals. Unlike the European liberals, Morelos wanted Catholicism to remain the only religion acceptable in his future state. The constitution made this point clear: "That the Catholic Religion is the only one, without tolerance of any other." Still Morelos called for the large landholdings owned by the church to be confiscated and given to landless people.

Freedom of Religion Today

For more than one hundred years after the time of Morelos, the Catholic religion was the only faith permitted in Mexico. Reformers continued to call for religious freedom, and the country finally attained that goal. Mexico is now governed by the constitution of 1917, which guarantees freedom of religion to all. Many protestant churches and some Jewish and Islamic houses of worship stand in Mexican cities today. Still, nine out of every ten Mexicans claim to be Catholics.

The constitution of Chilpancingo outlawed slavery and forbade the use of torture by police or courts. Although it did not address all the issues posed by Morelos, the constitution was one of the most progressive such documents written in the world at the time. The set of laws written at Chilpancingo represented the high watermark of the independence movement. But this amazing constitution inspired by Morelos never became the law of the land. The writing process was prolonged as congressmen debated endlessly over what often amounted to minor details. While the debates droned on, Spanish forces gained strength.

In February 1813, Spain promoted General Félix María Calleja to the office of viceroy. Authorities in Spain wanted their best—and most cold-blooded—military chief to crush the independence movement. The position of viceroy in colonial Mexico carried with it all the powers of the king of Spain.

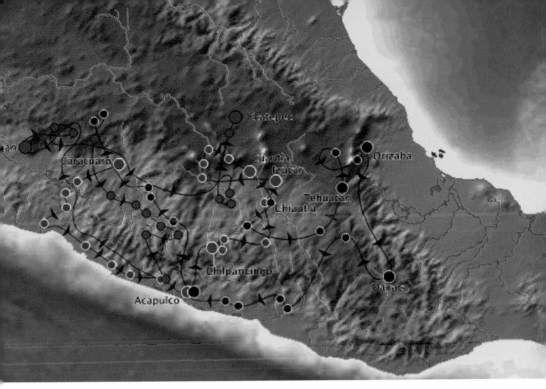

Campaigns of Morelos

Under the law a strong-willed viceroy could rule as a tyrant, and citizens of New Spain were powerless to object. Writer Justo Sierra said, "He [Calleja] symbolized and personified the policy of ruthless repression. Like many an agent of Spanish rule in Europe and in America, he believed in triumph through terror . . ."

Calleja strengthened his army by appointing mostly *criollos* as high officers. This was a dangerous move because *criollos* had led the early independence movement. But Calleja knew that since the massacre at Guanajuato the *criollos* feared an uprising of the dark-skinned lower classes. The new viceroy played on this fear and gained the support of some of the country's most important *criollos*.

Backed by the *criollo*-led army, Viceroy Calleja stormed into the rural areas torturing and murdering people while conducting a bloody counterinsurgency. Fear and cruelty

Antonio López de Santa Anna served under Calleja, helping him put down the liberal rebellion. *(Library of Congress)*

ruled New Spain. Justo Sierra said of these terrible times, "the countryside was ablaze with guerilla warfare . . . And, because the insurrection was being stamped out with heinous cruelty, the longing for liberty was whetted to a fierce desire for vengeance. It was a duel to the death."

In the north, Calleja's forces seized the vital silver mining towns of Zacatecas and Potosí. Calleja's royalist army then moved farther north to put down a liberal rebellion in the province of Texas. Hundreds of rebels were shot, including some early pioneers from the United States who had drifted west to establish ranches on the vast Texas plains. Serving with the royalist forces in the north was a young army officer named Antonio López de Santa Anna, who would later write his own bloody episode in Texas history.

Marching through the south the royalists took Cuernavaca and Taxco. At the town of Puruarán, the insurgent leader Mariano Matamoros, Morelos's "good right arm," was captured and shot. The royalists occupied Chilpancingo, where the constitution of the proposed new country was being written. Congressmen were forced to flee, and they blamed Morelos for his inability to protect them. Morelos accepted the blame. He offered to resign as commander and instead serve as a common soldier.

At Valladolid a force led by Morelos met a bitter defeat. His foe in that battle was the royalist officer Agustín de Iturbide, the same man who reported Hidalgo to Spanish authorities in 1810. Iturbide led a surprise cavalry charge which scattered Morelos's men. The defeat was an especially symbolic blow because Valladolid was Morelos's birthplace and the town where he first met Father Hidalgo.

By 1814 it was clear the insurgency led by Morelos was in a state of steep decline. Mexico itself was exhausted after suffering through three years of intense warfare. The colony's economy was in shambles: mines closed because workers had become soldiers, weeds grew on the untended fields of what had been productive farms, and hunger was common and devastating.

On November 5, 1815, Morelos was captured at the village of Temalaca. He was bound with ropes and placed on a horse for the long ride to Mexico City. Villagers along the route heard that the great man would be passing their way and everyone in the countryside lined the road to catch a glimpse of this heroic leader. General Calleja ordered hundreds of soldiers to guard his prize captive so no villager tried to free him. Instead the people stared in silence. As Morelos, tied up as if he were a bundle, passed by the onlookers bowed their heads. Many wept.

Father Morelos was tried first in a church court and then in a government court. The church tribunal found him guilty of heresy and excommunicated him. The government court charged him with treason and ordered him to be executed by firing squad. As his execution date approached, a group of jail guards, sympathetic to the independence movement, offered to free him and spirit him out to the countryside. Morelos refused, explaining that the act of fleeing would invite severe reprisals and the guards would be shot in his place.

On December 22, 1815, Morelos was taken to a dusty village outside Mexico City and executed by firing squad. Viceroy Calleja insisted the execution be carried out in a remote place to avoid demonstrations and possible uprisings. The viceroy hoped that the quiet death of Father Morelos would quietly end the Mexican war of independence.

But the voices crying for freedom would not be stilled despite the deaths of inspirational leaders such as Morelos and Hidalgo. As Justo Sierra put it, "independence, trampled, suffocated in blood, lived on in Mexican hearts."

NINE
The Collapse of the Spanish Empire

At its height the Spanish empire in the Americas stretched from the present-day U.S. states of Colorado and Utah down to Argentina at the tip of the continent. All of South America except for Brazil was part of the Spanish realm. In this era of colonialism, when Europeans worked desperately to carve out domains in less-developed parts of the world, rival European states envied Spain's vast holdings in the Americas. In the 1700s the English poet Samuel Johnson pondered the Spanish Empire and wrote:

> Has heaven reserved, in pity to the poor,
> No pathless waste or undiscover'd shore,
> No secret island in the boundless main;
> No peaceful desert yet unclaim'd by Spain?

For three centuries the flag of Spain waved over its huge territories on the other side of the globe. Spanish rule was often harsh, but it was firm. Independence was little more than a distant dream. Yet Spanish power vanished just ten years after the Enlightenment brought the spirit of freedom to the Americas.

South of Mexico two separate independence movements resisted Spanish authority. One independence program was headed by Simón Bolívar (1783-1830) who was born in Caracas, Venezuela. Leading bands of insurgents, Bolívar crushed the Spanish army in battle after battle. By the 1820s Bolivar won independence for the nations of Bolivia (which was named after him), Columbia, Ecuador, Peru, and Venezuela. Today Bolívar is called *El Libertador* (The Liberator) and "the George Washington" of South America. Farther south another crusading general, José de San Martín (1778-1850) who was born in Argentina, worked to free his region from Spanish rule. San Martín helped to liberate Argentina, Chile, and Peru.

The two independence movements in South America operated separate from each other. Bolívar and San Martín met just once, and then only for a brief period of time. Neither man worked in conjunction with the independence leaders of colonial

José de San Martín helped to liberate Argentina, Chile, and Peru.

Mexico. The fact that their movements succeeded can be traced back to disintegration in the mother country, Spain.

Spain was one of the least progressive nations in Europe. The king or the queen made and enforced the laws and the Catholic Church was the only church allowed. The church often acted as a nation within a nation by operating its own courts and fielding its own armies. Spain was a closed society, resistant of new ideas from the outside.

Then, during the eighteenth century, the Enlightenment stirred up passions in all of Europe and brought broad changes to the old order. In the summer of 1789, mobs of men and women marched through the streets of Paris chanting *Liberté, Égalité, Fraternité* (Liberty, Equality, Fraternity). It was the beginning of the French Revolution, a massive uprising by

During the summer of 1789, French men and women took to the streets to demand a change in government. *(Library of Congress)*

the lower classes against the kings and the aristocrats. Like thunder from a powerful storm, the winds of the French Revolution echoed over Europe. The old governments, which saw kings wielding absolute power over their subjects, collapsed in the wake of this storm.

Spanish leaders tried to insulate their people from the Enlightenment. Authorities banned books written by Enlightenment thinkers such as Locke and Rousseau, while the church threatened to excommunicate any Catholic who dared to read the radical works. But Spaniards defied church and civil authorities. They read the forbidden books in secret and passed them to their friends. Despite the efforts of the rulers, the concepts of the Enlightenment seeped into Spain.

As in Mexico, the Spanish people became divided into two political camps which were generally called the liberals and the conservatives. Liberals, driven by Enlightenment philosophies, moved to break the power of the monarchy and the church. Conservatives resisted all change and worked to strengthen the old system of kings and queens and a strong Catholic authority. The debate between the two sides weakened the government of Spain.

The liberal versus conservative debate rocked most of Europe in the early 1800s. With emotions burning like an out-of-control fire, war exploded on the European continent. The French Revolution, itself a product of the Enlightenment, brought Napoleon Bonaparte to power in 1799. Napoleon's armies, charged with the excitement of liberalism, spread out from France and attacked neighboring nations. Napoleon proclaimed he was a positive force of change in Europe, but in truth he hoped to carve out an empire devoted to his own

In 1799, Napoleon Bonaparte began conquering other European nations, building an empire for himself under the guise of revolution. *(Library of Congress)*

glory. Napoleon once said, "I love power as a musician loves his violin."

In 1808, French forces invaded Spain and won a quick victory. The Spanish king, Ferdinand VII, was sent into exile. Napoleon named his brother, Joseph Bonaparte, king of Spain. Spaniards revolted against French rule and a bloody guerilla-style war broke out. Spanish liberals led the guerilla forces against the French occupying army.

The Spanish resistance against Napoleon was called the Peninsular War, and it was fought on the Spanish Peninsula from 1808 until 1813. Spanish liberals were supported by England, Napoleon's most powerful enemy in Europe. In 1814, the French were finally ousted and the liberals introduced a new constitution for Spain that had been written in

This painting by Francisco de Goya depicts a scene from the Peninsular War.

1812. The document called for a return of King Ferdinand, but stipulated the king must share his power with an elected parliament. At first Ferdinand seemed to accept the power-sharing arrangement. Then, after reclaiming his throne, the king acted as an absolute royalist, dissolving the parliament and rejecting the constitution.

The liberals revolted against Ferdinand's rule, and unrest and civil war once more seized Spain.

Strife in the mother country produced a curious shift in political thought on the other side of the Atlantic. With Hidalgo and Morelos dead, conservative *criollo*s were left in charge of Mexico. In Spain the liberals were strong enough to oppose the king, and they seemed to be on the brink of taking power. But an ironic political change emerged:

Ferdinand VII

Spain, the mother country, was controlled by liberals who opposed rule by kings; Mexico, the colony, was led by conservatives who wanted to enhance the powers of the old monarchy.

The conservative viceroy of Mexico, General Calleja, sought to stamp out the liberal insurgents who still operated in his land. He removed from colonial government all men he suspected to be liberal sympathizers. His armies marched into the countryside, crushing any remnants of insurgent forces. In 1816, believing his mission in Mexico was accomplished, Calleja resigned as viceroy and set sail for Spain.

Upon arriving in Spain, Calleja raised an army and planned to march against the independence movements in South America. But Spain had changed while Calleja was in Mexico. The Spanish people were now charged with the almost electric energy of liberalism and they boldly defied commands issued by members of the old order. In 1820, the army Calleja was assembling rebelled. Spanish peasants, who were being drafted as foot soldiers, refused to die in the jungles and mountains of South America. Officers swore allegiance to liberal politicians instead of to their king. The liberals established a rival government, a junta (a word for group), and claimed the junta now ruled Spain.

Confusion in Spain united Mexicans with the belief that independence was now possible. All classes came to this conclusion even though they were motivated by different reasons. The church and the powerful *criollos* now pursued independence because they were dismayed by the liberal aspects of the Spanish junta. Mexican liberals were still inspired by the Cry of Dolores and pushed for independence as the proper idealistic conclusion of a long war. By 1820, all Mexicans desired independence. The only question debated was what sort of government a new and independent Mexico should embrace.

TEN

Iturbide and Final Independence

"I was always happy during the war," wrote Agustín de Iturbide as he remembered his service against the insurgents during the war of independence. "Victory was the inseparable companion of the troops I commanded. I did not lose one battle." He was not being boastful. Iturbide led soldiers into more than forty battles, including engagements against both Hidalgo and Morelos, and he won every clash against insurgent forces.

Personally brave on the battlefield, Iturbide was also one of the most brutal military chiefs in the Mexico of his time. He routinely shot prisoners and innocent civilians, tortured enemies, and burned villages which supported his opponents. Lucas Alamán, the teenager who witnessed the butchery at the Guanajuato granary building, said, "[Iturbide] was harsh beyond measure . . . [he] sullied his victories with a thousand acts of cruelty and the drive to enrich himself by any manner or means."

Agustín de Iturbide (1783-1824) was born, like Morelos, in Valladolid. His father was a wealthy *gachupin* and his mother a *criolla*. Some reports say his mother's family had mixed blood, and Iturbide should have properly been categorized as a mestizo. Iturbide hotly denied that any mixed blood tainted his heritage. Slim and always elegantly dressed, Iturbide became an officer in the Spanish-led militia at age twenty-two. Ambition burned in his heart. He knew military service was the best avenue of advancement for a young man in New Spain.

Agustín de Iturbide

During the bloody years of warfare between 1810 and 1820, Iturbide grew wealthy and powerful. In just a decade he rose in rank from lieutenant to general. One of his jobs as an army officer was to protect silver shipments which were made by mule train from the mines to the port of Veracruz. As a payment for his services he took a generous percentage of every silver shipment he delivered.

In 1820, Iturbide lived as a gentleman of high means in Mexico City. He was married, but he accused his wife of infidelity and forced her to reside in a convent. Freed of his wife, he courted handsome *criolla* women in the capital, and he indulged in gambling. His lifestyle soon cost him his fortune. Lucas Alamán, who knew him well, said, "[Iturbide] rapidly frittered away most of his wealth . . . leaving him in a very poor financial state."

While living in the capital, Iturbide made it a goal to acquire wealthy and influential friends. Some of those rich associates were independence-minded men who had supported the insurgents. Iturbide had few passionate political persuasions. He wished always to rise with the winning side. As Justo Sierra wrote, "he fought against [the rebels] because he believed the movement started by Hidalgo had no chance of success and thus no triumphant role for him to play."

By 1820, however, the times had changed. Spain was in a state of anarchy. Mexican independence, once an issue spoken of in whispers, was now openly discussed by liberals and conservatives. Iturbide sensed this shift in the political winds.

The Spanish Viceroy to Mexico in 1820 was Juan de Apodaca, who had been in office for four years. Apodaca was a devoted royalist who hoped the king would prevail against the junta in Spain. If the monarchy was reestablished in the mother country, he dreamed of the day when Mexico would return entirely to the Spanish fold. He wanted this return to be peaceable. Thus Apodaca offered amnesty to the few guerilla bands still working against the Spanish government. The most powerful rebel leader still fighting for independence was Vincenté Guerrero, the one-time lieutenant under Morelos. Though his forces were reduced, Guerrero still led a substantial army in the south.

To subdue Guerrero, the Viceroy called upon his most able officer: Agustín de Iturbide. Viceroy Apodaca did not like dealing with Mexican-born officers, such as Iturbide, because

Juan de Apodaca was the Spanish viceroy to Mexico in 1820.

he distrusted them. However most Spanish high officers had returned to the mother country, and he had no choice but to give the command to Iturbide. The viceroy explained his policy to put down the independence movement through forgiveness rather than military might. He suggested Iturbide try to negotiate with the rebel commander Guerrero, and offer him amnesty and freedom from punishment in exchange for disarming his forces.

In December of 1820, General Iturbide and a large army marched south into rebel territory. Though ostensibly following orders, Iturbide had plans of his own. He now dreamed of becoming the liberator of Mexico. If successful, he would win independence, stop the wars, and the grateful Mexican people would make him king or whatever office he desired.

Iturbide sent Guerrero a letter requesting a personal conference. They met and embraced while soldiers of both their armies cheered wildly. In February 1821, Guerrero and Iturbide concluded a series of talks in the town of Iguala, a place later made famous by a document called the Plan of Iguala. The Plan of Iguala, signed by both Iturbide and Guerrero, declared Mexico to be a separate and independent nation. Three hundred years of Spanish rule had ended. The Plan of Iguala was, in effect, Mexico's declaration of independence.

In addition to proclaiming independence, the Plan of Iguala presented an outline of future goals for the country. Three goals prevailed and they became known as the *trigarante* (three guarantees). The three fundamental guarantees were:

Mexican flag

gachupines and *criollo*s would become equal in the eyes of the government (mixed-race people were not mentioned), Roman Catholicism would remain Mexico's only religion, and Mexico would be independent from Spain. Article 16 of the Plan of Iguala read, "A protecting Army shall be formed, which shall be called the Army of the Three Guarantees."

Mexico's Flag

The flag of Mexico was adopted in 1821 and symbolized the three guarantees offered by the Plan of Iguala. It is a tricolor flag—green, white, and red. The green stands for independence, white for the purity of the Catholic Church, red for a union among the people. With only a few minor changes, that banner remains Mexico's flag to this day.

To spirited revolutionaries who fought with Hidalgo and Morelos, the Plan of Iguala was a disappointing compromise. It did not even establish Mexico as a republic. Article 4 stated, "Ferdinand VII or someone of his dynasty, or some other prince, shall become Emperor." Independent Mexico was to become a kingdom. The Spanish monarch Ferdinand or just about any European of royal blood was invited to sit on its throne.

Many of the other principals which inspired men and women to fight for independence were overlooked by the Plan of Iguala. It did not give rights to all races in accordance with the beliefs of both Hidalgo and Morelos. Progressive Mexicans wanted wording in their constitution to guarantee a free education for every child; education was not mentioned in the document. The Plan did spell out punishment for Mexicans who opposed its goals. According to Article 22, "Those who conspire against Independence shall be consigned to prison."

In Mexico City Viceroy Apodaca was aghast. He had sent Iturbide into the south to defeat Guerrero, and to advance the royalist cause. Instead Iturbide had conspired with Guerrero and declared independence. But there was little the viceroy could do to punish the scheming general. At this point the viceroy had few supporters, and the Plan of Iguala was written to appease powerful interests within the country. The church accepted the Plan because it established, "The Roman Catholic Religion, without tolerance of any other." Mexico's rich landowners were pleased with the clause that said, "All persons and properties shall be respected and protected." Even the royalists noted that, under the Plan, Mexico was to be a kingdom.

Iturbide reached out to the army, which had grown from 30,000 soldiers in 1810 to more than 80,000 in 1820. Most army commanders were *criollos* who acted more or less independently from authorities in Mexico City. Iturbide appealed to those men by offering them high positions in the future government. One after another, the officers joined the Army of the Three Guarantees and brought their regiments with them.

In April of 1821, Iturbide marched into Guanajuato, scene of the revolutionary slaughter some ten years earlier. This time Iturbide was greeted by the *criollo* General Anastasio Bustamante whose 6,000 men readily joined the Army of the Three Guarantees. A month later, Iturbide occupied Valladolid where even more officers and troops enrolled in the cause. To the south Vicente Guerrero and his ally, Nicolás Bravo, gathered armies and rallied behind the Plan of Iguala.

Much of this change went unnoticed in Spain. A one-way transAtlantic voyage took at least a month, and authorities in Spain were unaware of the growing acceptance of Mexico's latest independence movement. The liberal Spanish junta,

This drawing is a representation of a yellow fever epidemic. *(Library of Congress)*

which was more or less in charge of Spain, sent a new viceroy, Juan O'Donojú, to Mexico to replace Apodaca. The incoming viceroy arrived at Veracruz in July, 1821; he could not have come at a more unfortunate time. It was a hot, oppressively humid time of the year. Worst of all an epidemic of yellow fever had broken out in the Veracruz region. One-by-one men on the viceroy's staff and members of his own family caught yellow fever and some of them died horrible deaths.

O'Donojú was desperate to flee from the fever-ridden port city of Veracruz, but could not until he made peace with Iturbide. In August the viceroy met with Iturbide and agreed to accept the terms of the Plan of Iguala. For the first time ever a high-ranking Spanish diplomat signed a document granting independence to colonial Mexico. Leaders in the mother country were less disposed toward Mexican freedom, and it took fifteen more years for Spain to recognize Mexico as an independent state.

Iturbide chose September 27, 1821, to make his grand march into Mexico City; that date was also his thirty-eighth birthday. Residents of the capital loved celebrations and Iturbide gave them a carnival that would be talked about for years to come. Sixteen thousand soldiers of the Army of the Three Guarantees marched into the capital on a sunbathed morning. Riding at the head of this army was Agustín de Iturbide, mounted on a tall black horse, his saddle studded with diamonds and pieces of silver. Ahead of him bands played, church bells rang, fireworks exploded, and rockets pierced the sky. Elegant ladies wearing green, white, and red flowers in their hair—the colors of the Three Guarantees—stood on their balconies cheering and waving handkerchiefs. Lucas Alamán said of that glorious morning, "That September twenty-seventh was . . . the only day of pure enthusiasm and pleasure without any admixture of sad memories . . . that Mexicans had ever enjoyed."

The great fiesta of September 27 proclaimed to the entire world that Mexico was now and forever in the future an independent nation. It is ironic that Iturbide—a man who betrayed Hidalgo and brutally crushed the insurgent armies seeking independence—was Mexico's leader during this first celebration of freedom.

Liberals and idealists were disheartened by the course the nation took under the Plan of Iguala. Eleven years of warfare had cost the country dearly in blood. Some estimates say as many as 500,000 lives were lost in the fighting. But, at last, all Mexicans could now celebrate peace and freedom from colonial rule. As writer historian Justo Sierra wrote, "On September 27, 1821, the Army of the Three Guarantees made its triumphal entry into the capital of the Mexican empire. New Spain had passed into history."

ELEVEN
Viva Mexico!

After the great independence celebration Iturbide continued to win high praise in a country weary of war. He was called a "Virile Man of God" and the "Father of the Nation." A poet said of him, "It is you who have torn the mane of the Spanish lion to shreds." Intoxicated by this praise, Iturbide strengthened his hold over Mexico.

The Plan of Iguala established Mexico as a monarchy, and it called for King Ferdinand VII or some other European prince to take the thrown. Iturbide suspected from the beginning that no European monarch, least of all Ferdinand, would venture across the ocean to claim the country of Mexico as his realm. Mexico was a fledgling state, a country still at war with itself. A foreign king would be foolhardy to attempt to rule such a place. But a domestic king—one born in Mexico—was another matter. Iturbide envisioned himself as that special King of the Mexicans.

A congress met in February 1822. The congressmen were mostly *criollos* who were elected in a complicated process that limited voting to only the wealthy and the large land-owners. Iturbide assumed the role of the nation's president. At first the idea of Iturbide acting as president troubled few important Mexicans. He was already the de facto leader of the country and a national hero. It was widely assumed that Iturbide would graciously step aside if Ferdinand VII accepted the title of king.

In early 1822, the junta in Spain was overthrown and Ferdinand VII regained power. Ferdinand then made his intentions clear that he had no desire at all to become king of the Mexicans. No other European prince would claim the Mexican throne either. Iturbide's allies clamored to name him, Agustín de Iturbide, the monarch over a new country called the Empire of Mexico.

When asked to become king, Iturbide at first turned down the honor. Perhaps he wished to cultivate his image as a reluctant leader because people tend to distrust a person too eager to accept a position of power. Finally Iturbide bowed to what he deemed to be his civic duty and accepted the crown of Mexico. With a fine sense for drama Iturbide said, "I refused [the thrown] and finally consented in order to avoid evil consequences for my country."

On July 21, 1822, a formal coronation was held and Iturbide was crowned with great fanfare. Agustín Iturbide's official title was Emperor of Mexico; he announced he now preferred to be called Emperor Agustín I. Once more Mexico City was swept up in a rollicking party to celebrate the coronation. The rich went to fancy balls, and the poor sang songs around bonfires. But several observers at the coronation ceremony

In 1822, Iturbide was asked by congress to become the first emperor of the Empire of Mexico. *(Courtesy of The Granger Collection)*

noted that when a priest put the crown on Agustín I's head, it almost fell off. Was this near accident a sign of terrible fortunes ahead?

Post-independence Mexico was a country in name only; it had no unity. Indian people were more loyal to their individual tribes than to the nation as a whole. Several million Indians could not even speak Spanish. Mestizos still felt the burning frustrations of second-class citizenship. Whites remained divided between liberal and conservative leanings. The gap between rich and poor was enormous.

The Mexican silver industry was almost destroyed by the long years of warfare. *(Courtesy of The Bridgeman Art Library)*

After eleven years of war the Mexican economy was devastated. Silver mines produced only one-third the ore they turned out in 1800. During the war years, mobs damaged mining equipment and deliberately flooded shafts with water. The element mercury, which came from Spain, was essential in refining silver. Spain stopped mercury shipments to its rebellious colony and Mexican silver output diminished. Moreover the whole business community suffered because many merchants were *gachupines* who fled to Spain during the war. When they escaped the *gachupines* took bags of silver coins with them to the mother country. Fully half of the large farms were abandoned as Indians, the traditional farmworkers in New Spain, now refused to work for their *criollo* masters.

Thousands of poor people from the rural regions flooded into Mexico City in the years after independence. The most desperate of these impoverished masses became known as the *léperos* (the name comes from the disease leprosy although none actually had that malady). The *léperos*, who were so dirty they were thought to be untouchable, lived on the streets and survived by committing petty crimes and aggressivel

Destitute people from the rural regions of Mexico began flooding into Mexico City to beg and steal to survive. *(Courtesy of the New York Public Library)*

begging. Proper Mexico City families feared leaving their houses lest they be virtually assaulted by *lépero* beggars. Some wealthy city families even built alters inside their homes and paid priests to come and deliver private masses on Sundays because the simple walk to church was so harrowing.

Crowds of *léperos* haunted the shops and stood outside the doors of churches thrusting their open palms out to passersby. Many pointed to bodily wounds or other signs of sickness as proof they needed urgent help. A Spanish woman sitting on her Mexico City balcony described a *lépero* mob scene on the street below: "There come more of them! A paralytic woman mounted on the back of a man with a long beard. A sturdy-looking fellow . . . is holding up his deformed foot . . . What groans! What rags! What a chorus of whining!"

While the masses lived in bitter poverty, Iturbide's empire still supported a large army. Soldiers were paid in silver coins, each with a picture of Agustín de Iturbide stamped on its face. When the Empire of Mexico ran out of silver to pay the soldiers the government printed paper money for the first time in Mexico's long history. The paper currency was worthless. Merchants refused to exchange goods for the paper cash, and soldiers grew angry. Up until the currency crises the army had been Emperor Agustín I's staunchest ally. Now the poorly paid soldiers blamed their leader for their plight. Their bitterness was expressed in the words of a popular barracks song:

> I am a soldier of Iturbide
> And have seen the Three Guarantees.
> I stand guard in my bare feet
> And I go hungry every day.

Despite the country's financial ruin, Iturbide insisted on acting as a European king and displaying his personal wealth. He declared his title as emperor was hereditary and should pass down to his sons and daughters. He freed his wife from the convent, bedecked her with jewels, and the two took long carriage rides through the Mexico City streets. During such outings poor people and gangs of *lépe-ros* were paid a few coins to line the streets and cheer their emperor and empress. In private conversations Iturbide compared his life to that of France's Napoleon. Like the French leader, he thought of himself as a military genius who rose through the ranks and now devoted his talents to leading an empire. Congress spent more time establishing formal procedures for demonstrating the grandeur of the new emperor than addressing the major problems faced by the new nation.

Iturbide's pomp could not keep him in office while the underpaid military grew more rebellious with each passing day. Among the first to challenge the emperor was a highly ambitious junior army officer, Antonio López de Santa Anna, the commander of the Veracruz forces. He declared that he should take command of Mexico and that the country should become a republic, a nation without a king or any other inherited ruler.

Santa Anna had a long and stormy history with Iturbide. At first Santa Anna sent Iturbide cheerful letters congratulating him on becoming emperor. Santa Anna, then in his early thirties, even courted Iturbide's unmarried sister who was well past sixty. Iturbide distrusted Santa Anna because of his obvious ambitions and transferred him to an obscure post in Veracruz. There the exiled Santa Anna began plotting to seize power.

Post-independence governments of Mexico were characterized by military mutinies and proclamations. Typically a military strongman would gather his allies and his powerful officers together and "proclaim" a new government. Santa Anna's proclamation for a republic with him at its head was one of the earliest such moves. Vicente Guerrero and Nicholás Bravo joined Santa Anna in his effort to overthrow Iturbide and make Mexico a republic.

Iturbide sent an army to Veracruz to smash the rebellion. The army was led by General Echavárri, himself a calculating man who possessed a keen sense for which way the political winds were blowing. Instead of fighting Santa Anna the general joined forces with him. Together the two officers issued the *Plan de Casa Mata* which called for a republican form of government with a strong congress.

In Mexico City Iturbide knew he was defeated. In March 1823, he sent a letter to congress resigning from his position of leadership. His reign as emperor had lasted only ten months, yet he claimed the government of Mexico owed him 150,000 pesos (a fortune in those days) for expenses and pay. Iturbide never received the money and he left for Europe on board a British ship. A year later, Iturbide made the ultimate mistake of returning to Mexico. He carried bags full of paper money and printed proclamations heralding a new government with him in charge. He was returning because Spain planned to recolonize Mexico, and Iturbide saw this as an opportunity to rescue his country and redeem himself. But Iturbide did not know that congress had decreed he should be shot if he ever stepped on Mexican soil again. He was captured, and on July 19, 1824, the sentence was carried out in a small village near Tampico.

In November 1823, a new congress met to draft a constitution. The constitution created a federal republic similar to that in the United States. Mexico was divided into nineteen states and four territories. Each state enjoyed limited home rule. A noted exception to the U.S. constitution was that the Mexican document decreed Roman Catholicism to be the only religion allowed in the nation. The constitution also created a two-house congress, and it declared slavery to be illegal, though this aspect was not fully implemented until 1829.

In 1824 the various state legislatures elected Guadalupe Victoria the first president of the Republic of Mexico. Santa Anna had hoped to be the nation's first president, but at this point he lacked enough support to attain the office. Guadalupe

Victoria was a popular war hero who had followed both Hidalgo and Morelos in battles. He entered the war under his given name, Félix Fernández, but changed it to "Victoria" for victory in the war of independence and "Guadalupe" to honor the country's patron saint. The name was pleasing to the ears of the new nation.

In the early days of the republic, Mexico enjoyed a swell of national pride. Pictures of the Virgin of Guadalupe were posted everywhere. Praying to the Patron Saint was both a religious and a patriotic duty. Everything Spanish was denounced as foreign and ugly. Mobs in Mexico City threatened to break into the *Hospital de Jesús*, where the conqueror Hernando Cortés was buried, and dig up his bones and burn them. Priests in the hospital took the threats so seriously that they reburied Cortés's remains in a "secret place." That secret place went undiscovered until 1946 when it was found by researchers.

Laws were written protecting the Indians against discrimination, but the laws were largely ignored. In the decades after independence the Indians returned to living as farmers and suffering severe poverty.

Mexico remained an unstable country, especially compared to its northern neighbor, the United States, which had been thriving as an independent nation for some forty years. The U.S., under Great Britain, had always enjoyed some level of home rule; Mexico, under Spain, was allowed no such freedom. The Spanish government jealously guarded all institutions pertaining to its prized colony, and insisted all governmental decisions must be made in the mother country.

When Mexico finally became independent, civil wars and military uprisings continued to shake the country for the next one hundred years, as leaders with vastly differing views on the type of political and social system that should be put in place (liberal or conservative) maneuvered to take control.

While poverty abounded, the Mexican government supported a large army. Military payrolls absorbed about 80 percent of Mexico's budget. In 1825 the government collected 10 million pesos in taxes while its military expenses alone totaled 12 million pesos. Rich *criollos* were heavily taxed, and many had to sell their land holdings to meet their tax bills. Aggressive tax collectors even took the clothes off rich peoples' backs. Some *criollos*, driven to despair by taxes, committed suicide.

President Guadalupe Victoria borrowed from foreign governments in order to finance operations and meet the army payroll. This was a dangerous move. Foreign debt gave outside nations a ready excuse to invade Mexico and seize its assets. Those foreign interventions were another important reason for decades of instability.

At the time of independence the country was huge, stretching from what is now the southwestern United States down to present-day Guatemala. Much of that land, especially in the far north, had few Mexican settlers. The land-hungry United States looked with envy at these largely empty lands.

In 1828, Guadalupe Victoria's term expired. He was one of the few post-independence presidents to complete his legal term and peacefully allow himself to be replaced. Most other presidents were either overthrown by upstart generals or forced to resign because of political pressures. Another revolutionary war hero, Vicente Guerrero, took over as Mexico's second president. But waiting in the background was Antonio López de Santa Anna.

1838 map of Mexico

Santa Anna was born into a wealthy *criollo* family. As both a politician and a general he sided with Spain during the war of independence. When Mexico won its freedom he joined the patriotic flow and called himself a nationalist. Santa Anna readily switched loyalties between liberals and conservatives, always waiting to see which faction was stronger. A competent military leader, his troops usually achieved victory on the battlefield. Santa Anna encouraged friends to call him the Napoleon of the West.

In 1825 Spain sent military forces to Mexico in an attempt to regain its former colony. The Mexican government gave Santa Anna command of an army and ordered him to drive the foreign invaders off of Mexican shores. Spanish soldiers landed and occupied the port city of Tampico where many caught yellow fever. Santa Anna cleverly staffed his army with natives of the costal regions who were largely immune to the sickness. Fighting few battles, Santa Anna forced the weakened Spanish army to reboard their ships and sail back to Spain. He was then hailed throughout the nation as the Hero of Tampico.

The Hero and the Waiter

In 1829, while he was still riding the wave of popularity after his victory at Tampico, Santa Anna was given a testimonial dinner in the city of Oaxaca. Guests at the dinner were served by college students. By chance the waiter assigned to Santa Anna's table was a full-blooded Zapotec Indian who was studying law. Santa Anna noticed his waiter was barefoot. He was surprised that this young man, though he was a college student, was too poor to afford a pair of shoes. That youthful waiter was Benito Juárez who later became president of Mexico and tried to bring order to a nation that was being thrown into chaos because of civil wars and foreign invasions.

Santa Anna was named president of Mexico in 1833. He was unable to stop the civil wars, but he did manage to benefit from them. A skilled manipulator who changed sides frequently, Santa Anna was the country's president eleven different times between 1833 and 1855. When he did not hold high political office, he led the Mexican army in the field. The twenty-year period that ended in 1855 is often called the Age of Santa Anna.

In its first three decades of independence Mexico had fifty different governments. The presidents came and went in a bewildering succession of military coups and countercoups. One military strongman would declare himself leader only to be overthrown by another. During this confusing series of different governments, Antonio López de Santa Anna remained either the outright leader or the primary behind-the-scenes manipulator of the nation.

In the Age of Santa Anna the tragic war with the United States broke out. The region of Texas, in Mexico's northern frontier, was the focal point of the war.

Texas had long troubled the Mexican government. In the early 1820s Americans began moving into the region and claiming land there. At first Mexican leaders welcomed the American newcomers, provided they were willing to become Mexican citizens, learn Spanish, and convert to the Catholic religion. Only a handful of Americans complied with these terms. The large majority of American pioneers in Texas formed their own communities and lived as they pleased. In ten years more than 30,000 Americans had moved to Texas. The Americans, who called themselves Texans, far outnumbered the Mexicans living in the region.

Slavery and the Texans

Many American settlers in Texas came from the slaveholding states of Kentucky and Tennessee. The settlers brought their slaves with them when they migrated. The Mexican constitution of 1824 outlawed slavery. It was difficult to enforce the law in the far-flung province of Texas. The Mexican government issued orders telling the Texans to free their slaves, but the orders were ignored. American history books sometimes say the Texans broke away from the Mexican government because they desired freedom. One of the "freedoms" they fought for was their "freedom" to own slaves.

During the 1820s, many American pioneers began to move into the Texas region of Mexico to claim land there. *(Library of Congress)*

In 1835, the Americans living in Texas revolted and pronounced Texas to be an independent nation. Santa Anna, as the leading Mexican general, was sent to end this rebellion. On March 6, 1836, Santa Anna stormed the Alamo, an old church in San Antonio, Texas held by the American settlers. After a bloody battle, Santa Anna killed the force of about 150 Alamo defenders. Among the dead were the famous American frontiersmen James Bowie and Davy Crockett. Six weeks later a Texas army under the command of Sam Houston defeated the Mexicans at San Jacinto and captured General Santa Anna. During talks, Santa Anna agreed to recognize Texas as an independent nation in exchange for his personal freedom. Sam Houston complied, and released Santa Anna.

The news that Santa Anna had bargained away Texas shocked and infuriated the Mexican people. The government claimed Santa Anna had no right to cede Texas to foreigners, and it

The battle at the Alamo *(Library of Congress)*

refused to recognize the land transfer as legal. In Mexico City Santa Anna was denounced as a turncoat, a traitor, and a coward.

Santa Anna fell back on his incredible skill at self-promotion in order to regain the favor of the people. In 1838, General Santa Anna led a Mexican force against a French army which had taken over the port city of Veracruz. In the height of battle a cannonball hit Santa Anna and tore off his leg. Always cognizant of publicity, Santa Anna ordered a military funeral for the severed limb. Once more the Mexican people honored this brave soldier as a national hero.

From the beginning of their rebellion, the Texans who declared independence from Mexico wished to join the

United States. In December 1845, the U.S. Congress voted to welcome Texas into the union as the twenty-eighth state. This move to absorb Texas enraged the Mexican government. Texas was regarded as sacred Mexican soil, and no foreign power had a right to trespass on the region. Mexico ended diplomatic relations with the United States. The two countries exchanged angry letters. War loomed.

The United States in the 1840s was gripped by an almost religious spirit called manifest destiny. The term was coined in 1845 by a newspaper editor named John O'Sullivan who wrote, "[It is] the fulfillment of our *manifest destiny* to overspread the continent allotted by Providence for the free development of our yearly multiplying millions." Simply put manifest destiny was the belief that God willed the American people to expand from the eastern states and absorb all the territory to the west. No force on Earth could prevent this expansion.

The United States, with its burgeoning population and adventurous pioneering spirit, was destined to spread from the Atlantic to the Pacific.

The prime architect of manifest destiny was President James K. Polk, who took office in 1845.

James K. Polk *(Library of Congress)*

Polk was most interested in annexing California, then Mexican territory. Sprawling in-between the established United States and California was the huge area called Mexico's northern frontier. This land, which includes today's states of New Mexico and Arizona, was little known to the Americans. Nevertheless the land had to be conquered if the aims of manifest destiny were to be served.

In April 1845, President Polk sent an American army in Texas south to the Rio Grande River. In effect, Polk was declaring the Rio Grande to be Texas' southern border with Mexico. Even by manifest destiny standards this was an arrogant move, as the traditional Texas border was farther north, along the Nueces River. On April 25, Mexican and American soldiers clashed in a region near Matamoros. A furious President Polk told Congress, "Mexico has passed the boundary of the United States, has invaded our territory and shed American blood on American soil."

On May 13, 1846, the United States Congress declared war on Mexico. The Americans attacked overland from the north and from the sea after landing in Veracruz. The Mexican army was superior in numbers, but was poorly equipped and poorly led. Post-independence mutinies and infighting had weakened all Mexican institutions, including the military. Even Mexico's best general, Santa Anna, was unable to rally his men to victory. Mexican soldiers failed to win a single battle during the war. In the late summer of 1847 the Americans marched into Mexico City and raised their flag over the capital.

On February 2, 1848, American and Mexican officials signed the Treaty of Guadalupe Hidalgo officially ending the war. For Mexico, the terms of the treaty were disastrous.

Depiction of Santa Anna fleeing from American soldiers *(Library of Congress)*

Mexico was forced to cede all of its northern frontier and California—a total of some 525,000 square miles—to the United States. The loss of California was particularly grievous because just months after the treaty was signed gold was discovered there. Thousands of eager miners flocked to California, and the once sleepy region enjoyed a fantastic economic boom.

At the time of independence Mexico was a land giant, comparable to Russia, China, or Brazil. As a result of the Mexican-American War, Mexican territory was cut in half. Because of this tremendous land loss, the newly independent nation was gripped by a feeling of gloom.

After the war with the United States, political confusion continued in Mexico. Taking advantage of the situation, Santa Anna seized power in 1853. He ruled as a dictator without even the pretense of democracy. Santa Anna now preferred to be called His Most Supreme Highness. The country was in grave political and economic disorder, yet Santa Anna spent his efforts designing new uniforms for army officers and building fancy carriages for officials, the same mistakes made immediately after independence by Iturbide.

Benito Juárez, a poor, full-blooded Zapotec Indian, went on to become president of Mexico. *(Library of Congress)*

In 1855, Santa Anna was overthrown and forced to move to Venezuela where he owned a ranch. The ex-dictator was allowed to come home in 1872. By that time Santa Anna was impoverished due to failed investments and gambling debts. He was once one of the richest and certainly the most powerful man in Mexico, but he died almost penniless in Mexico City in 1876

Santa Anna's brief regime was the last time a major figure from the independence-era led Mexico. It was as if Santa Anna's ultimate fall marked the final end of Mexico's war of independence.

On the surface it appeared the independence movement produced little more than war and turmoil. For a century after independence Mexico remained an unstable nation. It was not until the late 1920s that Mexico developed a firm government.

But to deny the positive results of the Mexican independence movement is to do a disservice to the people who fought and died for freedom. In 1821, Mexicans achieved their independence, and thereby broke three hundred years of Spanish domination. Furthermore Mexicans established their character and their national identity during the independence struggle. As Justo Sierra said, "[Mexico] was born during the eleven years of [independence] conflict in the same way every nation is born: by becoming aware of itself."

Timeline

1519 Fleet of Spanish ships under the command of Hernando Cortés lands at Veracruz.

1521 Cortés and Spanish army conquer Aztecs.

1531 According to legend, the Virgin of Guadalupe appears before a humble Indian peasant name Juan Diego; the Virgin of Guadalupe becomes the patron saint of Mexico.

1540s Silver discovered in central New Spain; the colony eventually becomes the world's largest silver producer.

1650 Mestizos, a new race created by the blending of European and Indian bloodlines, make up about 20 percent of New Spain's population.

Early 1700s The *Enlightenment*, also called the *Age of Reason*, begins in Europe.

1776 The United States declares independence from Great Britain.

1789 The French Revolution begins in Paris.

1799 Napoleon Bonaparte takes power in France.

1803 Father Miguel Hidalgo y Costilla is named parish priest for the town of Dolores in central Mexico.

1808–

1810   French armies conquer Spain.

September 13—Key members of the Literary Society of Querétaro arrested for plotting independence movement.

September 16—Hidalgo begins the war of independence with speech, which later became known as the *Grito de Dolores*.

September 28—The battle for the city of Guanajuato begins.

October 30—Hidalgo's army defeats Spanish at the Battle of Monte de las Cruces; Hidalgo chooses not to march on Mexico City.

1811   March 21—Hidalgo arrested.

July 30—Hidalgo executed by firing squad.

December—New independence leader Father Morelos commands an army of 9,000 and controls much of southern Mexico.

1812   February—Spanish general Calleja surrounds the town of Cuautla, where Morelos is headquartered; siege begins.

May 2—Morelos leads his forces out of Cuautla, escaping Calleja.

1813   Morelos assembles a congress at the town of Chilpancingo, declares independence, and begins to write a constitution for the new land.

1814   French armies driven out of Spain.

1815   November 5—Morelos captured at the village of Temalaca.

December 22—Morelos executed by a firing squad.

1816 Calleja returns to Spain.

1820 An army recruited by Calleja to fight South American insurgents revolts.

1821 February 24—Agustín de Iturbide issues the Plan of Iguala, proclaiming independence and presents rules for a future government.
September 27—Iturbide, leading the Army of the Three Guarantees, marches into Mexico City and establishes independence.

1822 Agustín de Iturbide named Emperor of Mexico.

1823 General Antonio López de Santa Anna proclaims Mexico should be a republic; Iturbide is driven from office, escapes to Europe.

1824 Guadalupe Victoria becomes the first president of the Republic of Mexico.

1833 Antonio López de Santa Anna becomes president of Mexico for the first of eleven times.

1835 Americans living in the Mexican province of Texas revolt.

1836 Santa Anna storms the Alamo in San Antonio, Texas, killing the American defenders there.

1845 U.S. Congress accepts Texas as the twenty-eighth state; Mexican and U.S. armies fight in Texas in April.

1846–

1848   War rages between Mexico and the United States; Mexico is defeated and looses all its northern territories—some 525,000 square miles.

1855   Santa Anna, who had been ruling as a dictator, is overthrown.

Sources

CHAPTER TWO: New Spain

p. 14, "the most beautiful thing . . ." Hugh Thomas, *Conquest: Montezuma, Cortés, and the Fall of Old Mexico* (New York: Simon & Schuster, 1993), 517.

p. 14, "The city looked as if . . ." Hammond Innes, *The Conquistadors* (New York: Alfred A. Knopf, 1969), 193.

p. 15, "The Indians were so trampled . . ." Enrique Krauze, *Mexico, Biography of Power: A History of Modern Mexico 1810-1996* (New York: Harper Collins, 1997), 35.

p. 17, "They died in heaps . . ." Jonathan Kandell, *La Capital: The Biography of Mexico City* (New York: Random House, 1988), 154.

p. 18, "We are very busy . . ." Krauze, *Mexico, Biography of Power*, 34.

p. 26, "We are surrounded by . . ." Kandell, *La Capital*, 214.

p. 27-28, "It rained poets . . ." Justo Sierra, *The Political Evolution of the Mexican People* (Austin, Texas: University of Texas Press, 1969), 127.

p. 29, "Listen to me with your . . ." Kandell, *La Capital*, 224.

p. 29, "intellect formed by the . . ." Sierra, *The Political Evolution of the Mexican*, 128.

CHAPTER THREE: The Enlightenment

p. 35, "Counter to all . . ." Gilbert M. Joseph and Timothy J. Henderson, ed., *The Mexico Reader: History, Culture, Politics* (Durham, North Carolina: Duke University Press, 2002), 161.

p. 38 "All property and wealth . . ." T.R. Fehrenback, *Fire and Blood: A History of Mexico* (New York: Macmillan, 1973), p. 281

p. 40, "Every pulque tavern . . ." Kandell, *La Capital*, 259.

CHAPTER FOUR: Hidalgo

p. 49, "a man of ideas . . ." Sierra, *The Political Evolution of the Mexican People*, 150.

CHAPTER FIVE: The Battle of the Banners

p. 52, "Indians' mother of God," Sierra, *The Political Evolution of the Mexican People*,153.

p. 53, "Liberty for these . . ." Ibid.

p. 56, "I am at the head . . ." Douglas Richmond, *The Mexican Nation* (New Jersey: Prentice Hall, 2002), 105.

p. 57, "[A Spanish officer] ordered his soldiers . . ." Joseph and Henderson, *The Mexico Reader*, 182.

p. 58, "The insurgents, after taking . . ." Ibid., 183.

p. 60, "I am a true Catholic . . ." Fehrenback, *Fire and Blood*, 328.

p. 60, "In any case . . ." Sierra, *The Political Evolution of the Mexican People,* 154.

p. 64, "pardon is for criminals . . ." Ibid., 332.

p. 64, "stared straight at us with . . ." Krauze, *Mexico, Biography of Power*, 103.

CHAPTER SEVEN: Morelos

p. 76, "bad weather and little profit," Krauze, *Mexico, Biography of Power*, 105.

p. 76, "the best church . . ." Ibid.

p. 76, "He yells at us . . ." Ibid.

p. 76, "they are very much . . ." Ibid.

p. 77, "I am a miserable man . . ." Ibid., 105-106.

p. 77, "totally ready to sacrifice . . ." Ibid., 106.

p. 78, "change one's heart," Ramón Eduardo Ruiz, *Triumphs*

and Tragedy: A History of the Mexican People (New York: W. W. Norton & Company, 1992), 157.

p. 78, "our campesinos . . . who tilled it," Ibid.

p. 78, "[We must] overthrow . . ." Joseph and Henderson, *The Mexico Reader*, 190.

p. 81, "Entire villages keep wanting . . ." Krauze, *Mexico, Biography of Power*, 107.

p. 82, "calm, without excitement . . ." Ibid., 108.

p. 82, "good right arm," Fehrenback, *Fire and Blood*, 336.

CHAPTER EIGHT: The Dream and the Defeat

p. 88, "servant of the people," Fehrenback, *Fire and Blood*, 338.

p. 88, "That America is free and . . ." Joseph and Henderson, *The Mexico Reader*, 189.

p. 88, "That sovereignty springs from . . ." Ibid., 189-90.

p. 89-90, "That the Catholic religion . . ." Ibid., 189.

p. 91, "He [Calleja] symbolized and personified . . ." Sierra, *The Political Evolution of the Mexican*, 161.

p. 92, "the countryside was ablaze . . ." Sierra, *The Political Evolution of the Mexican People*, 156.

p. 94, "independence, trampled, suffocated in blood . . ." Ibid., 161.

CHAPTER NINE: The Collapse of the Spanish Empire

p. 95, "Has heaven reserved . . . " Samuel Johnson, "A Poem in Imitation of the Third Satire of Juvenal," Literature Network, http://www.online-literature.com/ samuel-johnson/3246.

p. 99, "I love power as . . ." Will and Ariel Durant, *The Age of Napoleon* (New York: Simon and Schuster, 1975), 242.

CHAPTER TEN: Iturbide and Final Independence

p. 103, "I was always happy . . ." Krauze, *Mexico, Biography of Power*, 121.

p. 103, "[Iturbide] was harsh beyond . . ." Ibid.,122.

p. 105, "[Iturbide] rapidly frittered . . ." Ibid., 123.

p. 105, "he fought against [the rebels]," Sierra, *The Political Evolution of the Mexican People*, 167.

p. 108, "A protecting army shall be . . ." Joseph and Henderson, *The Mexico Reader*, 194.

p. 108, "Ferdinand VII or someone . . ." Ibid.

p. 109, "Those who conspire against . . ." Ibid., 195.

p. 109, "The Roman Catholic religion . . ." Ibid., 194.

p. 109, "All persons and property . . ." Ibid.

p. 111-112, "That September twenty-seventh was . . ." Krauze, *Mexico, Biography of Power*, 124.

p. 112, "On September 27, 1821 the Army . . ." Sierra, *The Political Evolution of the Mexican People*, 169.

CHAPTER ELEVEN: Viva Mexico!

p. 113, "Virile man of . . . lion to shreds," Krauze, *Mexico, Biography of Power*, 125.

p. 114, "I refused [the throne] and . . ." Ibid., 126.

p. 117, "There come more . . ." Kandell, *La Capital*, 297.

p. 118, "I am a soldier of . . ." Krauze, *Mexico, Biography of Power*, 127.

p. 128, "[It is] the fullfillment of . . ." Ralph K. Andrist, ed., *Making of the Nation: 1783-1860*, 231.

p. 129, "Mexico has passed the boundary . . ." Ibid., 260.

p. 132, "[Mexico] was born during the . . ." Sierra, *The Political Evolution of the Mexican People*, 176.

Bibliography

Andrist, Ralph K., ed. *Making of the Nation: 1783-1860.*
New York: American Heritage Publishing Company, 1987.

Durant, Will, and Ariel Durant. *The Age of Napoleon.*
New York: Simon and Schuster, 1975.

Fehrenback, T.R. *Fire and Blood: A History of Mexico.*
New York: Macmillan, 1973.

Harvey, Robert. *Liberators: Latin America's Struggle*
For Independence. New York: Overlook Press, 2000.

Innes, Hammond. *The Conquistadors.* New York: Alfred
A. Knopf, 1969.

Joseph, Gilbert M., and Timothy J. Henderson, eds. *The*
Mexico Reader: History, Culture, Politics. Durham,
North Carolina: Duke University Press, 2002.

Kandell, Jonathan. *La Capital: The Biography of Mexico*
City. New York: Random House, 1988.

Krauze, Enrique. *Mexico, Biography of Power: A History*
of Modern Mexico 1810-1996. Translated by Hank
Heifetz. New York: Harper Collins, 1997.

Parks, Henry Bamford. *A History of Mexico.* Boston:
Houghton Mifflin, 1969.

Richmond, Douglas. *The Mexican Nation.* New Jersey:
Prentice Hall, 2002.

Ruiz, Ramón Eduardo. *Triumphs and Tragedy: A History*
of the Mexican People. New York: W. W. Norton &
Company, 1992.

Sierra, Justo. *The Political Evolution of the Mexican*
People. Austin, Texas: University of Texas Press, 1969.

Thomas, Hugh. *Conquest: Montezuma, Cortés, and the Fall*
of Old Mexico. New York: Simon & Schuster, 1993

Web sites

http://www.mexonline.com/mexican-indepdence.htm
This online guide to Mexico includes a page on the history of
Mexican independence.

http://www.inside-mexico.com/featureindep.htm
Inside Mexico is a comprehensive source of books, music,
videos, and cultural articles about Mexico in English and
Spanish.

**http://www.tsha.utexas.edu/handbook/online/articles/
MM/qdmcg.html**
The Texas Historical Association, in conjunction with the
General Libraries at the University of Texas, Austin, provides
an article on the Mexican War of Independence on this site,
the *Handbook of Texas Online.*

Index